MW01230240

An Average Guy's Journey to
Becoming a Millionaire

An Average Guy's Journey to Becoming a Millionaire

A Guide to Exiting Debt and Becoming Wealthy

Written By a Millennial

Jeremiah DeCuir

Edited by Michele Decuir
Written by Jeremiah Decuir

ISBN 979-8-9866833-0-0 (Paperback)
ISBN 979-8-9866833-1-7 (E-book)
ISBN 979-8-9866833-2-4 (Hardcover)

Table of Contents

Foreword

The goal of this book is to answer one question. How? How did you become a millionaire? How is it possible to become a millionaire in this day and age when the cost of living is so expensive? How do you become a millionaire when culture teaches us to work, work, and work some more until we feel like all of our hopes and dreams are killed by our reality to simply survive? We get caught in a vicious working schedule, possibly doing something we don't even enjoy, only to make ends meet month after month. How do you fight this? How can someone with an average upbringing break free into a life they always dreamed?

This book will answer these questions. It is the story of Jeremiah and Stephanie Decuir. Our upbringings, our schooling, our marriage, our working lives, and our lives together. It will answer the question of how to become a millionaire.

The short answer to this question, I will answer here in the foreword. The longer answer is the entirety of this book. Every financial book I have read has always contained at least one

golden nugget of information that I have found helpful. This book is no different because we are all at different points in our lives and careers. Sometimes the information we need is right in front of our faces, and we simply need reminding. Other times we are learning
something new for the first time. Either way, I hope you find many golden nuggets for yourself within these pages.

The short answer. How do you become a millionaire?

Planning, hard-work, diligence, never giving up, more diligence, getting back up when you have fallen down, sticking to the plan, and crossing the finish line.

In a few more words, here is a breakdown of this short answer.

By planning, I mean to have a GOAL. Set a goal, make a goal, to do what YOU want. You can do and be anything you want. So, what do you want? I answer this question very simply. I WANT TO BE A MILLIONAIRE. That is my goal. That is what I have committed my body, soul, and mind to achieving because I believe it is best for me and my family. So, what do you want? What do you believe is truly best for you? Your answer may not be the same as mine, and that's okay. But I encourage you to go after what you want with all you have! Never give up!

By hard-work, I mean to make money. To get it done! To become a millionaire I need money, more money than I have currently until I either have a million dollars, or my net assets total to one million dollars. I can't become a millionaire if I don't have money, so I'm going to get to work and keep all the money I make so that it will one day total one million dollars. This sounds simple enough, but it's not. That's why diligence is so important.

By diligence, I mean to stick to the plan. Do NOT get distracted. See this thing through until its achieved. Don't let anyone get in your way, especially yourself. After 3 years of working a crappy job that pays okay, but that you don't care for any longer, CAN YOU STAY DILIGENT? Can you find a way to suck it up? Or at the least find another job? It's in this stage, that you will find out how bad you really want IT. Whatever your IT is. During this stage, you will find out if you ACTUALLY want the goal you have set for yourself. Most people fizzle out during this stage, because any goal worth achieving will take multiple years to complete. If it wasn't difficult to complete, then everyone would do it. So, how bad do you want IT?

Preface

At the time of writing this book, my wife and I are not millionaires (see how I snuck the word *journey* into the title there). However, we do have a net worth over $500K, it's just not up to one million, yet.

At this point in our lives, it would take a truly catastrophic event for us to not hit the million-dollar mark within the next 5 to 10 years. We have set up our lives to automatically increase this number every month without us changing our daily habits. We do this through automatic retirement investing, paying the mortgage on time with additional principal payments, and investing into a stock brokerage account with low-risk mutual funds. It's on autopilot essentially. No big schemes, no big hustles, and no big lottery ticket buys. It's kind of boring really.

I have no doubt in my mind however, that if I keep automatically doing these things month after month, our net worth will inevitably reach one million dollars. It's not a question of how to become a millionaire anymore for us, it's a question of when.

Once you get the ball rolling down the hill, you get to stand at the top and watch patiently as it accelerates towards the bottom. This is exactly how I feel right now. I'm just waiting. I've pulled out a lawn chair, watching the clouds roll by with a glass of sweet tea in my hand.

The ball is starting to roll faster and kick up more dirt as we pass each $100K mile marker. Occasionally, the ball gets slowed down by a boulder in the way or the stock market taking a downward tumble. But now that the ball has crossed the $500K marker, it has so much speed that it's going to make it to the bottom of the hill one way or another as long as I don't try to stop it.

I hope that one day, you get to feel this way. It's pretty satisfying. I want you to know that you can become a millionaire! Everyone can become a millionaire! You only have to begin by carrying your ball to the top of the hill. You can do it!

Chapter I: The Structure of this Book

Each chapter of this book will give me and my wife's personal experience, followed by the major financial, intellectual, or the personal lesson we learned from it. I will always relate this lesson we learned back to money and our goal of achieving millionaire status. The first chapters are the beginnings of our lives, both separately and together. While the last chapters are where we are today on our journey in becoming millionaires.

I will try to be direct and not waste your time with extra words in this book. Financial literacy is very basic. There is no secret sauce to becoming wealthy overnight, unless you are one of the statistical anomalies that win the lottery or inherit a bunch of money. If you are one of these anomalies, this book is not for you. Statistically, less than 1% of the US population will become millionaires for these reasons. I am not a part of that 1% and more than likely, neither are you.

My qualifications to write this book are nada! All of the content in this book is a combination of personal financial education and self-reflection on our individual experiences. While my wife and I have bachelor's degrees from formal universities, a college education is certainly not necessary to becoming wealthy. Our college experiences did shape our view on money and school debt as you will see. The true value of going to college for us was to learn how to learn and think for ourselves. That concept has shaped the content of this book more than anything.

At the back of this book, I have included a list of other financial books that I used to become educated on the subject of financial literacy. They are listed in order of importance for my life. You might have a different opinion as to their order; however, they all offer a piece of some useful financial information. When read together as a whole, they are like putting puzzle pieces together into a bigger, financial literacy picture.

On the topic of Dave Ramsey. If you do not know who he is, I highly suggest you do a quick Google search of him. I believe Dave is awesome because he has helped so many people! If you struggle with credit card debt, have expensive car loans, and/or struggle with just providing basic needs for you and your family month to month, I highly recommend starting with Dave Ramsey's content. No one on the planet has a higher track record for leading people out of debt. I encourage you to complete his baby steps 1-3 at minimum while reading this book. You will view this content through a different lens by doing that. Your mind will be able to think more freely because you won't be worried about trying to solve your day-to-day money problems.

Chapter 2: The "Secret to Life"

The first step to becoming a millionaire happens inside your mind. Just like deciding to exercise more or go on a diet, deciding to focus your attention and energy into growing your net worth is the same concept.

If you could go back in time and teach your freshman high school self-one thing, what would it be? For me, I'd teach myself something I refer in my own head as the "secret to life". It's not 42, and it has nothing to do with any religion-based philosophy. It's much simpler. "The secret to life" for me is deciding to do something and finding a way to get it done, no matter the sacrifice.

For example, I played baseball for my high school many years ago. I used to think that talent was something you were born with. Now I know without a doubt that had I truly applied and committed myself to baseball, I could have been very good. Committing myself meant fielding ground balls every day. Like a basketball player needs to shoot 100 free throws every day, I needed to take 100 swings of the bat every single day. To be the greatest first baseman, I needed to dig 100 low balls out of the dirt without letting them get by every day. To be the best pitcher I needed to throw 100 pitches *every day*. I needed the commitment of diligence AND the diligence of commitment in order to surpass my peers in their *talent* and become the best baseball player I could be. While my peers may have more natural talent than me to play baseball, I would have easily surpassed their natural talent by deciding to out-work them and to commit to my growth in the game more than them.

There is a second part to the "secret to life" that is equally as important as my baseball example. In order to swing the bat 100 times every day, I'd estimate that to be a time commitment of 1-2 hours per day. I would have to give up other aspects of my life during those 1-2 hours, that other people do not. I would have to sacrifice my time every day in order to become a great hitter. During those 1-2 hours, I wouldn't be doing schoolwork, or hanging out with friends, chasing girls, working on cars with dad, playing videogames, skateboarding, sleeping, working, doing chores, OR ANYTHING ELSE. I am sacrificing relationships with friends, parents, potential spouses, my grades at school, making money, learning a new skill and catching up on sleep all by deciding to hit 100 baseballs per day. This is SACRIFICE! It's the major secondary concept to the "secret to life" after deciding to hit 100 baseballs per day.

Just like brushing your teeth every day keeps cavities away, swinging a baseball bat 100 times a day for 6 months, 1 year, 5 years will automatically make you good at hitting a baseball because you do it SO MUCH! You will learn things that other people do not by being so familiar with the action of swinging.

Your muscles build and adjust to exactly what you need to hit the ball effectively. Your mind internalizes the fluid motion of the swing and makes it a normal motion like walking. You will automatically become better at hitting the baseball over anyone else who doesn't swing the bat at least 100 times a day. This is the "secret to life". This is the secret to being good at ANYTHING in life.

Sports are the easy analogy, but the "secret to life" expands much further outside sports. For example, someone who wants to become an architect needs to either go to college to study architecture or study with someone who is already an experienced architect. To be a well-known author, someone needs to write something every day in order to become a better writer and study the skill of writing. To become a professional trumpet player, someone needs to play the trumpet every day for many years (possibly decades) in order to one day land a spot in a professional symphony. To lose 30 pounds, someone has to prioritize exercising, managing calories and committing to the goal of losing weight. And to become a millionaire, one must organize and prioritize the activities of their life in order to learn to save and invest their money until they achieve millionaire status. THAT is the "secret to life".

You already know the things to do and not do if you want to be a millionaire. The formula is do not give your money to other people. Keep it for yourself. For example, put money in a savings account. Save for retirement. Don't buy cars, houses, or go into debt for any reason. Your mind already knows these things! Simple, right?

Unfortunately, life is not that simple. Our lives are complex with children, activities, work, sleep, vacation, the list goes on. But our lives can be simplified in our own mind with some focus. Just like deciding to go on a diet for 3 months, you can decide to focus on growing your net worth for 3 months. It's the same thought process.

If you want to become a millionaire, YOU must decide that YOU actually want to be a millionaire. It's that simple. It's not magic, and it's not going to fall in your lap someday. Some people live their whole lives believing that one day, they will be rich. They turn 65, 70, 80 still believing that someday something good will happen to them that makes them a millionaire. Then someday, they die and that's it. They die in debt with nothing to leave to their children except the stress of the family having to pay for a funeral.

This is the sad truth of what most families go through. But it doesn't have to be YOU! YOU can decide this will not be you TODAY! Don't die and leave you closest family members to figure out how to bury you! That's something I would do to my enemy, not the ones I love! So don't do it. Decide right NOW

Chapter 3: The Past and The First Step

When I was six years old, my parents divorced. My younger brother and I grew up with my mom who took full custody of us. Both my parents were very civil with each other, and we grew up seeing our dad about 2-3 times a month normally on the weekends.

So the story of a struggling single mom working a full time job to support her two young children was definitely my story growing up. My dad did pay a substantial amount of child support every month to my mother, so that was truly the only way my mom had any chance to make ends meet. Despite the child support, I can clearly remember making trips to my grandmother's house (my mom's mom) every so often, where I realized my grandmother would give my mom a check for a few hundred dollars to make it through a month sometimes. Looking back now, my mother worked her tail off and did all she could to support two small children in the best way she knew how. I am very proud of her for that.

However, observing certain situations where I realized my mother was completely stressed out worrying about how to pay for food, clothes, the mortgage, utilities, and the car was something that took a toll on me as a child. I very clearly remember being in my first-grade classroom where I made a conscious decision that I would NEVER turn out like that. I would NOT EVER be worried about money when I grew up. I saw the stress on my mother and our family, and I knew I did not want that. Sometimes you learn best by watching someone excel at something like your favorite athlete in a sport you love. Other times you learn by watching what not to do. The latter was definitely the case for me when observing my mother handling money.

So, in first grade, I very clearly remember having my first encounter with the "secret to life". What can a first grader control or do to ensure they aren't poor when they are older? The answer now I would give you is "not a whole lot". A first grader doesn't really have a lot of control over their life at that age. They are more interested in recess and riding their bike outside when they get home from school, of which I was no exception.

But my answer back then was much more straight forward and clear, just like the mind of a first grader. Every little kid about my age probably heard from their parents "get good grades so you can one day go to college and get a good job". It's only now, many decades later, that society is seriously beginning to question this advice due to the skyrocketing cost of higher education. However, that was not what my first-grade brain heard. Literally, my brain heard this advice and internalized it as "good grades = college = high paying job". I watched my mother struggle and knew I would not ever be like that. So I focused on almost the only thing a little kid can focus on. Getting good grades in school.

From first grade, all the way through high school, I can count on one hand the number of B's I received on my report cards. And I can assure you, I didn't receive my first C in any class until I got to college. So, you can guess what the rest of the grades were. They were straight A's down every report card during my entire childhood. Any parent would be proud, and both my parents certainly were, but I'm not entirely sure they understood WHY I had straight A's until many years later when I told them. I was not competent enough to voice this accurately to my mother until after I finished college. But I did understand it in my own head because I remember making that commitment to myself in first grade to get good grades. That's where it started. It ended with me finishing as salutatorian in my high school class of about 650 graduating seniors.

I was not special, talented, gifted, or a genius. I simply listened to the advice of my parents, committed myself to schoolwork, and therefore got good grades. I studied and worked my ass off in high school to do well because of the commitment I made to myself. Said another way, my reasoning and commitment to myself drove me to do better than six hundred and forty-nine of my peers. In the words of Dave Ramsey, my "why" was bigger than theirs. And my sacrifices to get there were bigger than the other students around me.

It's only looking back on this years later that I can fully recognize what I sacrificed in order to get straight A's my whole life. Straight A's don't magically appear on a report card because you're smart. They appear because you put in more hours on homework, school projects, extra credit, writing school papers, and studying for tests even when you don't feel like it. Just like a baseball player needs to take 100 swings of the bat every day, I spent extra time to put forth my best efforts in all schoolwork. I was not scared to ask questions in class to the teacher or a peer; nor was I the annoying kid asking excess questions seeking a teacher's attention. I was trying to understand whatever concept they were trying to explain, because that's what I needed to get the grade. I was focused for many years.

Here is one very small and very specific sacrifice I remember making back then. In 2007, Halo 3 was first released. I can remember being super excited for it coming out. A buddy of mine and I waited in line to be one of the first to get it at midnight. We got it and played it for hours on end into the early hours of the morning. However, I can't tell you that I played much more of Halo 3 after that night. While I can assure you that I did play it on and off for a year, I never let that game, or any game distract me from the commitment I made to my schoolwork. I HAD to get good grades so I could one day get a high paying job. That's what I remember today, not the hours and days of my life that I spent playing Halo with my brother and our friends. School work always came before Halo. I sacrificed more video game time in order make sure I did well in school.

I know what you're thinking, Boo Hoo! Poor kid didn't get to play Halo. He sacrificed SO much to get good grades (huge eye roll). To this, I would say you are both right and wrong. The list of sacrifices that one makes to achieve a goal is endless and many times small in nature, especially when made over a long period of time. Sometimes the timing and grand total of many small sacrifices can greatly outweigh the weight of larger sacrifice someone makes in one moment. On the other hand, most high school kids don't actually have any real, major responsibilities like a mortgage payment, car payment, insurance, gas, groceries and utilities to worry about. So, as a sophomore in high school, I can definitely remember a cool new video game being very high on my priority list as a teenager. It took up a larger portion of my time and attention, probably more than it needed to.

To weigh the responsibilities of a teenager with those of an adult is not a valid comparison. Said another way, what a teenager in high school has to sacrifice is MUCH less than what an adult has to sacrifice. Teenagers compete with the other six hundred and forty-nine students in their graduating class. Adults compete with all other adults, even those that are much older than them. Teenagers worry about getting their driver's license. Adults worry about feeding their new 3-month-old. Teenagers worry about if their crush is going to be at the party Saturday night, while adults figure out how to pay the rent this month. Teenage and adult sacrifices are NOT the same. For a teenager to stand out, they only have to sacrifice to the extent that the other six hundred and forty-nine teenagers did not for their grades. This is a very small sacrifice compared to anything an adult worries about.

The Lesson

My need to get good grades was the result of hopelessness. Not my own hopelessness, but my mother's. While this type of motivation is not ideal, especially for a first grader, it was very effective. The belief that I would one day be able to take care of myself and my mother is what drove me to do well in school.

Hopelessness exists in many forms. In my mother's case, it was a vicious cycle of getting up to go to work every day to a 40-hour week job, taking on the stress of that job, coming home to house chores, taking care of two boys each evening; and still not being able to pay all the bills after working SO DAMN HARD consistently for years. Her only true relief was getting to sleep in on Saturday mornings for as late as possible.

If you can relate to this, I am very sorry for the hopelessness you feel. It's real, and you are caught in a vicious cycle of which you must break. This is an absolutely crappy way to live. I do not wish this torture upon my worst enemy.

The hopelessness you feel month to month from rent, mortgage payments, car payments, electricity, water, food is an individual emotion. The United States is the greatest country on Earth AND the RICHEST. When you go to a baseball game, Disneyworld, on a cruise, golf tournament, on any vacation ever; you generally notice that the people around you are genuinely happy to be there. If you don't feel that way almost every day of your life, then you may be fighting the hopelessness I'm describing. Forming a plan and executing that plan to exit the hopelessness is the first step to becoming a millionaire.

The good news is that this hopelessness you feel is only a state of mind. IT CAN BE BROKEN. You must find a way to make progress to exit your hopelessness. It is truly the first steps to believing and becoming a millionaire. The act of forcing your mind to exit and enter different states of mind is a useful skill, and it's not easy. To view the world in a positive, glass half-full, endless opportunity state of mind is relieving, encouraging, and wonderful.

Each one of us has the ability to get up in the morning and make different decisions that put us on different paths. The question is, what are you doing today to make one small step of progress towards exiting the mindset of hopelessness? Just like the baseball player who takes 100 swings a day, what are you doing today to make your life better? The answer to this question is different for each person. For example, some people want to open a business, or start a new career, or have a family, or find a spouse, or make more money, or disappear into the Rocky Mountains. Each of us is different, but you must start by answering this question for yourself.

However, if your response to this question is that you will do nothing towards exiting your current state of hopelessness, then congrats. It should come as no surprise that you will continue to exist as you are. Doing the same thing you are doing today will not make a difference. So DO IT! GET UP AND

Jeremiah DeCuir

DO SOMETHING! GET OUT THERE AND CHANGE YOUR LIFE! GET OUT THERE AND MAKE STUPID MISTAKES AND TRY AGAIN AND AGAIN! No one else is going to change your life. IT'S YOUR LIFE!

Chapter 4: College Life and Lessons

After graduating high school in June of 2009, I went on to college at Texas A&M in College Station studying aerospace engineering as my major in the fall of 2009. While that sounds cool, I can assure you it was awful. I felt like a hot shot kid that could do anything with my good work ethic and study habits. I was very wrong! Every single freshman class, calculus, physics, and engineering intro in particular knocked me on my ass and into reality! Your straight A student in high school became a straight C student that could barely get by. I was devastated. I realize now that it was only because of my work ethic and study habits built from high school that I pulled out C's in all my classes. I was missing something major, and I had yet to find what that was.

If you find my school commitment made to myself in first grade a bit strange, I wouldn't hold that against you. In relation to how this commitment had an effect on my college life however, I can totally understand if you think I'm a weirdo based on what I'm going to say next. My college experience was very different than most because of my personal views on life and this first grade commitment I made to myself. For example, I did not drink one drop of alcohol while in college. The only time I had ever tried an adult beverage was when I was about 7 years old. My dad let my brother and I have a taste of his beer. To this day, I remember how disgusted I was and how horrible it tasted. My brother felt the same. This stuck with me all through college. I am thankful my dad shared his beer with me so young. I will one day do this with my own children.

Next on the list of personal choices that shaped my college life, I did not attend a single college party all four years. No frat parties, no ring dunks, not a single, traditional college get together like those that are popularized on TV. I was a working hermit, except for attending college football games. That was my one outlet that I enjoyed every fall semester. My study schedule completely revolved around the A&M football team's schedule. I took my schoolwork very seriously, studying for tests, working on assignments, and homework. I was not about to let alcohol, girls, or partying mess up what I had been working for since first grade. I had way too much invested in myself to screw it up now.

That being said, I can't describe to you my level of devastation in becoming a straight C student. I did not handle it well, and I did some serious soul searching because I knew I was letting myself down. I just couldn't figure out how and why it was happening. I wasn't partying or doing any of the traditional college distractions, and I was studying A LOT!

It's only looking back, that I can fully answer this question as to why I struggled so bad. It was a combination of many things. Many of these points directly correlate to the life habits of what it takes to be a millionaire. My main problems were as follows:

First, I was not using my study time effectively. I was not developing systems for studying like making notecards, taking practice quizzes, or working practice problems over and over again until I could do them in my sleep. Reading and highlighting chapters of a book were not effective for me, even when done 3 times over. I had to discover my personal learning preferences and put those into practice for each class. This took me 2-3 semesters in college to fully understand and be able to get better grades. I will come back to this point later because I truly believe this is one of the most valuable lessons that college has to teach any individual on the planet. I had to learn how to learn and utilize my time to maximize the information I could retain.

Second, I had lost some of my personal motivation after finishing high school. I had lost my why. I had achieved getting into college, so moving on to the next step towards finishing college wasn't something I had wrapped my brain around just yet. Also, that first-grade commitment was not enough anymore to outperform my peers. I was suddenly competing with multiple thousands of students instead of only 650 in my high school. Not only were there more people, but they all had at least some form of personal motivation close to my first-grade commitment as a base foundation. At minimum, we were all paying a premium to attend a university, so a grotesque amount of money can motivate almost anyone to do anything. My point is, I had not raised the bar for myself and my motivation level past that of my first-grade self. What did I need to do every day that my classmates did not or refused to do in order to make sure I achieved an A? And what was my reason for doing this? I had yet to answer these questions.

Third, I had almost no time management skills. In high school, this almost takes care of itself because there is a bell ringing all day enforcing you to move on to your next class. After school activities were easy to manage too because they generally went 1.5-2 hours after school and stopped before the late buses arrived. College was different. There are no bells at any time, and the campus was huge! Sometimes I needed a bike or a bus just to shuttle me between different class locations. Thus, time and energy is required to learn bus routes and schedules to ensure that the bus doesn't make you 20 minutes late for class. For me, the bus routes were the start of developing those time management skills.

In addition to my school difficulties during this time, I decided to introduce a new wrinkle into my life that was something I had never done before. I officially started dating a girl I went to high school with in January of 2010. Right after my first horrible semester, she became the brightest light in my life that I looked forward to every minute of the day. The only issue with our relationship was that she was in Denton, Texas at Texas Women's University, about four hours from College Station.

Now before your brain starts judging me about the difficulties of trying to have a long-distance relationship, I'll start by telling you that I ended up marrying this woman and our 10-year anniversary is in June of 2023. When something works, it works, and we both decided individually that we wanted to find a way to make things work between us. For me, deciding to commit to a relationship was the second major time in my life that I decided deep in my soul that I was going to fully commit to something. The first time was in 1999 as a first grader. The second time was in January 2010. My "secret to life" now became something adaptable and applicable to a wider range of subjects that included personal relationships. It took me 2-3 years to realize that committing to a personal relationship and committing to grades are very different, yet they share a common core belief of personal commitment. While they are different, they are still the same.

That being said, my wife Stephanie and I had a few major helpful keys that spurred our relationship along. The first was that Stephanie's parents lived in Clifton, Texas. Which if you don't know, happens to be EXACTLY between Denton and College Station. This busting metropolis is a one stop light town with a population of 3500 people. It just happens to be a two-hour drive both from College Station and Denton. (I know, like I said, when things work out they work). So on many weekends, Stephanie and I were able to see each other 3-4 times a month.

The second major key to our relationship is that Stephanie's grandmother lived in Bryan, Texas. The cities of Bryan and

College Station are essentially connected at the hip, even more so than Dallas and Ft. Worth. My dorm was a 10–15-minute drive to her grandmother's house depending on traffic. So, Stephanie always had a place to stay in College Station when we would go to football games or go on dates. My dorm room was not suitable for both Stephanie, me and my roommate to try and share such tight living quarters.

On top of all of this, Stephanie's family grew up in Bryan. She had aunts and uncles that had gone to A&M at one time or another. All of Stephanie's aunts and uncles, including her mother, grew up in Bryan for their childhood. Her family was well connected to the area (not in a financial or political way, but in a personal, regionally centered kind of way) which had an effect on me after we had been dating for a few years. By the time I was senior in college, College Station felt like my second home partly because I got to know Stephanie's side of the family so well. They welcomed me into their family, probably more than they know, and I am overly grateful to them to this day.

Stephanie and I dated in this long-distance manner through our sophomore years. After that, Stephanie had the opportunity to continue her college studies to become a nurse in Houston, Texas. Her final two years were spent living in the medical center of Houston. Coincidentally, downtown Houston is a two-hour drive from College Station. So, for our entire college dating life, we were always about that far from each other. By the time senior year rolled around, I had found a rhythm of busting my ass during the week for 60+ hours, studying and working my part time job, so that I could hang out with Stephanie on the weekends. She became one of the reasons I needed to get my crap done during the week, which upped my personal motivation game.

The Lesson

As I said, building up my personal motivations and developing the skills I needed for college took me 2-3 semesters to finally get the hang of. After my first semester, my answers to these questions and skill developments were implemented as follows for the rest of my college career. These things built me into the person I am today, and I'm not sure that I would have learned these lessons had I not attended college. While I fully believe college is NOT necessary to learn these lessons or achieve millionaire status, it is important that you find SOMEWAY to learn these basic skills. ANY way you do this is perfectly acceptable! These have been my specific examples of how I absorbed these teachings through my own personal experience. Hopefully, you can relate to something I have written here. Everyone learns differently and has different experiences, so *your* experiences need to shape your life and guide you towards making tomorrow better for yourself. The following are the things I did to get my act together and earn better grades in college:

First, I spent study time making absurd amounts of notecards for classes when I was required to learn new vocabulary, dates, formulas or any factual information that I didn't know. After creating the notecards, I would constantly quiz myself during every free moment I had on a bus, between classes, during lunch etc. Also, I spent a huge amount of time working calculus, statics, thermodynamics, and engineering work problems over and over and over again until they either made sense, or I could memorize the problem solution sequence well enough to get most of the credit. Lastly, I spent copious amounts of time working previous tests that many professors shared freely with all students. If a previous test existed, I worked that sucker for hours and hours in the days leading up to a major exam. Those three activities forced me to maximize my study time.

More important than these specific details of what I did to maximize my study time, is the process in which I developed to succeed. The process of making notecards, working practice problems and old exams many times over is what my brain needed to achieve the highest levels of my professor's' expectations. As an example, instead of making notecards, a welder may need to spend a weekend making a welding jig that makes his life easier for a certain job he performs a lot. Another example might be a plumber who needs to make a tool or keep his inventory stocked and organized in the work truck so that all his jobs run smoothly when a customer calls. Finding that tool or developing that organizational process that helps you achieve the tasks at hand is what must be done to make yourself successful. Even if that means spending a little money or shrinking your free time.

By the time my last semester rolled around, I was almost bored with implementing this same system to each class. I already knew I was going to get an A because I had discovered my individual winning formula. Developing an individual winning formula that fits your life AND increases your net worth every month is a key to becoming wealthy.

Second, what I did every day that my peers did not was study effectively in every means available to me. I found that, especially as I entered my sophomore year of college, some of my classmates would get derailed in their own motivations, close to what I had experienced my first semester. However, they continued to allow their new college freedoms to blossom into full on life habits. Some were developing bad habits for drinking too much, partying, chasing girls, sleeping etc. When they were hung over from the night before, I was studying and putting in the work developing my own positive work habits to combat against even the people who could party hard and still pull off good grades. While I envied people that could do this, in the long run, I knew my positive working habits would beat them.

Hard work consistently built over many semesters of positive habits turned into me finishing my senior year with two 4.0 semesters. I treated studying as if I had a full-time job. I easily hit 40 hours of work time per week especially including time in class. More realistically, I was closer to 55-60 hours per week spent in class and studying.

Third, my answer to time management was sticky notes! I know that sounds weird, but my sophomore year, I started planning my days in 30-minute increments from 6 AM until 10 PM. I would fill up a tiny sticky note with details of bus route times, class times, lunch time, study time, exercise time, random daily tasks, and bedtime. I made one sticky note each evening for the next day's activities so I could get up and go each morning at 6AM. If something wasn't written on my sticky note, I didn't do it. Each day was carefully planned down to each 30-minute increment so that I could maximize the daylight. I stayed committed to the sticky notes, and they rewarded me with a highly effective time management skill developed by my senior year.

This skill was compounded and perfected after I took on a part time job for an oil company in College Station the summer before my junior year. I was required to work 18-20 hours per week at their office that was on a bus route ten minutes from campus. Sticky notes were my life saver for managing my daily activities! Otherwise, I would not have had enough daylight hours to be a full-time student and hold a part time job for my junior and senior years.

I point these things out, because these solutions and skill sets developed over time are what has made me confident that I will one day achieve millionaire status. These ideas and skills must be adapted towards saving, investing, and making money, but at the core they are still the same principles that can make anyone a millionaire.

I'm not saying you need to have a sticky note written out each day in 30-minute increments for yourself. But I am saying you need to have a plan each day as to how you are going to make progress towards your goals. Even if you're only able to devote 1 hour each day towards achieving that goal. If you don't find a way to put in your time to progress that goal each day, then do you actually deserve to achieve it? I stuck to the schedule those damn sticky notes gave me, and I didn't let distractions derail me from following my day's plan.

Chapter 5: Where Real Life Started

For you nerds out there looking for some numbers, this chapter is for you! I'm going to dive into the financial details of me and my wife's college debts, cash, salaries, bonuses, and random things we paid for with actual numbers. I hope you've enjoyed the accelerated story telling of my life so far. We have successfully made it through my childhood and graduated college to this point. Now that the stage is set, we get to really dive into the good stuff of what it takes to be a millionaire!

In 2013, my life was packed! In May of 2013, both Stephanie and I graduated from college with bachelor's degrees. On June 1st, 2013 Stephanie and I got married! On June 10th, 2013 I started working full time for the oil company I had been working part time with for the last 2.5 years. It was a crazy couple of months!

We finished college with a combined debt of about $80K which was about $800 dollars a month in minimum payments! Yikes! This number still gives me a little anxiety just thinking about it, however at the time, we knew we were very normal.

Just about all of our peers who went to college with us had about the same amount of debt or more. 2013 was such a big year for us that I remember not being worried about anything else except settling into a place of our own, starting a new job, and enjoying being married. Eighty thousand dollars seemed like an insurmountable amount of money at that time, so why worry about it? There was nothing we could do about it then (or so we believed).

Now the part that is FULLY anxiety ridden is the $800 minimum payment. At the time, this payment was enough to afford a *really* nice car; like a fully loaded Mercedes or Cadillac SUV. As of now writing this, an $800 monthly payment still buys you a very nice car, but it's not enough to afford the type of SUV I'm describing back then. The only reason Steph and I weren't scared out of our wits about this $800 minimum payment was that I already had a full-time job lined up in Houston making $70K per year with a $15K signing and relocation bonus (before taxes). We didn't exactly know what the monthly check would be, but we knew it was more than enough to cover this $800 payment plus our living expenses. So life continued on, and the anxiety of school loans completely went over our heads both fortunately and unfortunately.

I can only claim this to be an unfortunate event looking back on it. The analogy I would give you is that the gates of life were opened to us after marrying and finishing college, however all we did was join the herd of cattle in the pasture that ALSO had as much debt as we accumulated and ALSO thought it was no big deal. We were all simply one big herd, chewing the grass every day and living a normal life. Had we seen this $80K of school debt as more of a burden after we married, I can assure you that our net worth would be MUCH closer to the million-dollar mark today.

Regardless, we viewed our life during this time as wildly grateful, happy to have each other, and blessed to enter the real world as adults. We didn't require ANY support from either of our parents anymore, and we were proud of that for ourselves. Don't get me wrong, we still feel this way today, however it's in a wildly different way than how it felt back then. Here are a few more details I'll share with you to give you a complete picture of our financial life at this time.

I worked various jobs from the time I was 16 all through college during summers and winter breaks (at a BBQ restaurant, a band instrument repair shop, and part time for an oil company as you know). I made on average about $5K each summer I worked after taxes. I estimate that I made about $35-40K total from when I was 16 years old until I was 22. Through those various jobs over many years, I ended up with enough saved my senior year in college to be able to pay cash for Stephanie's diamond ring ($5K), payoff a truck that Stephanie owed about $2K on, and pay for our honeymoon after the wedding ($4K). I also had about $3K still saved, but this would slowly get drained because I had to make a $400 truck payment out of it until my first paycheck came from the new job.

Now, where the rest of the money went that I saved from my summer jobs, I have no idea! I didn't track any of my financials back then or have any kind of budget, so I can't tell you where it went. I suspect it went towards, gas, car insurance, restaurants and a small car note I had in high school. But all of that doesn't add up to the missing $21K-26K that I'm talking about.

Here is a complete snapshot of what our net worth was back then immediately after finishing college. The definition of net worth is all assets added up minus all liabilities subtracted out. Calculating this is surprisingly simple for anyone coming out of high school or college because THEY DON'T HAVE ANY MONEY, most of time. Calculating net worth becomes significantly harder as more assets and liabilities enter the picture. But here was our net worth in June of 2013:

Assets		Liabilities		Net Worth
Item	Value	Item	Value	
Stephanie's Truck	$12K	Jeremiah's Truck Loan	$-9K	
Jeremiah's Truck	$15K	Jeremiah's Student Loan	$-25K	
Savings Account	$3K	Stephanie's Student Loan	$-55K	
Checking Account	$200			
Total:	$32.2K		$-89K	$-56.8K

We had a negative net worth! Meaning the world had spotted us almost fifty-seven thousand dollars just to live our lives to that point! Does the fact that your life may actually have a negative, monetary net worth freak you out a little? I can tell you; it certainly didn't bother Stephanie and I back then. We were happy cows enjoying the company of our new adult herd that we had just been granted access to. The grass was green, the sun was shining bright, and the pond out in the pasture was teeming with fish.

Life was blissful then! Stephanie and I felt hugely rich! I came out of college thinking we were set for life making more money than both my parents had ever made during any point in their working careers! I believe Stephanie felt the same. To get your first paycheck, and be able to easily pay the rent, student loans, gas, utilities, groceries, out to eat, and have about $500 left over which we could save was huge! Our monthly gross after health insurance, retirement, and taxes were taken out was just over $4000 dollars. Here was the breakdown of our monthly expenses back then:

Monthly Expenses - 2013	
Monthly Paycheck	$4000
Rent + Utilities (2 Bed/1 Bath Apartment)	-$1350
Minimum Student Loan Payment	-$800
Groceries & Restaurants	-$450
Truck Note	-$400
Gas & Car Insurance	-$300
Cell Phones, TV & Internet	-$200
Leftover Money	**$500**

I remember thinking that working for my company was a huge blessing! And it was! I remember being grateful to the point that I would do almost anything for my employer. That salary afforded a lifestyle for my wife and I that neither of us had ever grown up with. Both of our households had always struggled with money in different ways. And to be able to break free from that was such a huge relief! I remember feeling like a partial load was lifted off my shoulders over a period of a few months after I realized that my company would continue paying me again and again. Even if I took vacation time, they would still pay me! It felt like we had won and beat the system that seemed to be against us even though I was too young to understand what system that even was!

While we did set aside a few hundred dollars every month into savings because we figured it was the "right thing to do", I realize now that we had absolutely no clue about money. We were simply a newly married couple who enjoyed cooking dinner each night while tuning in to our favorite TV shows and falling asleep each night with a bowl of ice cream polished off for dessert. Life was good! But things were about to change for better and for worse in the coming years. It's only now that I look back and realize that it was during these blissful first years of marriage that we established some unhealthy money habits that were not catastrophic, but didn't help us to progress towards millionaire status either.

The Lesson

We didn't see our debt as problem. We didn't view our negative net worth as a problem. We were just enjoying living life as adults. We had our own apartment. We were eating what we wanted. And we were going anywhere we wanted. We were just existing, enjoying the moment without any real regard for the future. We were happy cows.

In the short term, there is nothing wrong with enjoying each and every moment of your life. However, this mind set can be dangerous if you never seek to partially exit this state of mind. Being a happy cow with the new herd is fun for a while, but you are still a cow. Enjoying every moment is important but finding and taking the next step is as equally important towards giving even more value to your life, your family, and your friends. It is certainly a multi-tasking situation.

I'll give you a hint as to what happens next in the story. It's something that pops my nice little fairy tale I've laid out for you. What happens to that nice cushy job at the oil company when suddenly they can't make a profit to save their life? What happens to our lives when something completely out of our control happens? What do you do? Unexpected events happen to everyone in life, so how are you preparing today for tomorrow's unknown? We definitely were not prepared for what life had in store for us next.

Chapter 6: Saving For a House

By August of 2013 we found a groove just living a very normal life and enjoying a normal routine.

Steph finished nursing school in May of 2013 from Texas Woman's University. She didn't have a job lined up yet because she hadn't taken her official test to become a certified RN at that point. She was very focused on studying and passing her RN test within the next month, while I went to work at a very steady 9-5 job every day. We ate good food and made a few purchases we had always wanted (like a 50" TV). We lived as we both envisioned what married life to be. We were very happy, content, and grateful for our current lives.

On top of this contentment, we both were looking forward to something that we knew would materialize by the end of the year. Steph was very likely going to get her first nursing job within a few months! She was very nervous about passing the RN exam because it was her last obstacle to becoming a real nurse in the hospital setting. She had been hesitant to apply for jobs until she passed the test because she had wanted to be able to state her license number on her resume to employers in order to prove to them that she had already passed the test before even interviewing. (Looking back at it now, this actually wasn't too big a deal for her and potential employers. Nurse managers normally have a set number of new graduate nurses they can take on each year. Passing the RN test for someone who already received a BSN in Nursing is much easier to accomplish than someone who doesn't have that 4-year degree. Not to say it can't be done, it's just easier. Also, having a BSN in Nursing is WAY more valuable to hospitals in general, especially for hospitals that seek different accreditations).

After all her studying and nerves, Steph passed the RN test her first try in September of 2013! Woo!!! Life just kept getting better for us it felt like!

Shortly afterwards, she applied to many hospitals in the Houston area and went on several interviews over the next month. Eventually she was hired as a floor nurse in a medical-surgical (medsurg) unit at St. Luke's Hospital in the Woodlands. I was so proud of her! Our families were incredibly happy and proud for her! By the end of 2013, she had officially started her nursing career on a new unit that St. Luke's was opening. It was the perfect experience for a new nurse looking to start out.

So now, financially, you can imagine things are REALLY looking up for us. It was breath taking the amount of money we were about to be making. Steph's starting salary was about $50K a year before taxes. We now had a dual income household making $120K that year coming out of college together!

While that combined salary is crazy for any recent college graduates, we luckily hadn't built any horribly, unhealthy money habits by that point. We were splurging on a few minor items we always wanted like a PlayStations, Wii, and other crafts and electronics. We were slowly building up a hefty tolerance for fine dining like Ruth Chris's steak house, and other overpriced restaurants, but we still hadn't made any major purchases like on cars or vacations. I think we were both happy at home and hungry to get to work to learn new things at our jobs. We were excited to go to work! Who wouldn't be when you get paid like we were AND get to join major corporations in the adult world.

In addition to this we had begun talking about buying a house in the near future. With our income, we knew it made sense for us to make progress towards that. We already had about $10K saved and thought we were loaded! We were proud of that, and it was a lot of money to us. However, adding Steph's salary into our lifestyle seemed too good to be true. We already had so much and could buy whatever we wanted. A combined income of $120k coming out of college just seemed ridiculous!

Ultimately, for the next 8 months we decided to save her entire income. Her take home pay was right at $3500 a month (she didn't have health insurance coming out of her check like mine. It was cheaper for us both to be on my company's insurance back then). We saved so much money so quickly in that time frame. It was shocking!

At the end of that 8 months is the start of where things went awry for us regarding spending habits and financial literacy. We had saved about $25K on top of the $10K we already had in savings. A few things stand out to me now that I want to point out.

First, we had a goal. We were saving to buy a house. We saved up more than enough for a 5% down payment on a conventional loan for a $300K house. Looking back, setting the goal together to save to buy a house was a good decision. However not saving at least 20% for a down payment was not our brightest plan. Had we stayed in an apartment for 1 more year we would have easily saved for the 20% down payment. Avoiding paying private mortgage insurance is well worth it in most cases. It was ESPECIALLY true for us because our income was high enough to save more than 20% within a year.

Second, our school loans were not the priority AT ALL. We certainly made the minimum payments, but in our minds, buying a house was WAY in front of trying to pay down student loans. We both agreed on this without discussing it much at all. We were full steam ahead on saving for a house down payment, just like many of the other cows in the pasture.

The Lesson

The power of two people setting out to achieve a goal together is something not to be overlooked. To this day, I am super proud of us for saving so much money so quickly for the goal of purchasing a home. We worked together, combined our finances, got to work, and knocked it out of the park in 2014.

Two people working a plan together is a powerful tool when they are fully invested into that plan. This should not be underestimated. The best way I can describe this is that studies have shown that people live longer lives when they have a life partner. Whether they are married or not, is not really important. What is important is that you have a partner that shares life with you both emotionally and physically. When two people intentionally make plans, set goals, and work to achieve those goals together; they grow together and make each other better humans along the way. In general, they are also happier. This is the reason I believe that married people live longer lives than single people statistically speaking.

Money has almost nothing to do with this concept of the power of two. The only place money comes into play is that personal finances are a direct reflection of the state of you and your partner's lives. How you handle money with your life partner is a reflection of both your good and bad personal, emotional, and physical habits. Your checking account transaction history (or credit card transaction history) will automatically reveal bad habits to an outsider upon visual inspection. They will also reveal positive habits in the same way. Money is neither good nor evil, it is simply a reflection of you and your partner's state of mind and thus, your happiness with your own lives.

Chapter 7: Stuff Happens

This is the part where you get to make fun of me for being an idiot. Things were too good to be true in our lives. We certainly felt that way, but it didn't actually click in until a few years later in 2016 when the price of oil took a global nosedive. We aren't quite there yet, but I'll get to it.

In the summer of 2014, Steph and I moved into a brand-new house we built on the northeastern side of Houston. We were thrilled! This house was almost 3000 square feet and was plenty big enough to grow into if we decided to have children in the future. Our plan had been to skip over the starter home phase so that we would possibly stay in this new house for at least ten years.

I laugh at myself for this proposed future plan now. Any young person in their twenties WILL NOT live in the same house for ten years. Something will happen in their lives that requires a change. Whether it be getting married, having children, starting a new job, moving/relocating to a better job, losing a job, family crisis etc. The list goes on for reasons that people move and sell their homes.

While living in a brand-new house was awesome, the monthly payment on this house was NOT awesome. Because we only put 5% down, our monthly note was $2600. To compound this problem, our property taxes significantly increased in 2015 because of our house being finished in the middle of the previous year. So, the mortgage company reassessed our mortgage, like they do every year, but our monthly payment increased to $2850 in 2015 in order to afford a full year's worth of property taxes. There was nothing we could do about this, but we were not prepared for such an aggressive jump in our monthly payment so quickly. It was a live and learn situation.

Here's a breakdown of our monthly finances in 2015. Regarding our income, we had both achieved at least one yearly pay bump by the standard 3% that most employers give each year to all employees. I'll also note that our gas bill went up significantly after we moved. We both had longer commutes to our jobs because we were anticipating my company to move locations within the next two years close to our new house. I've adjusted for these things in the breakdown below:

Monthly Expenses - 2015	
Monthly Paychecks	$7700
Mortgage	-$2850
Utilities + HOA	-$500
Minimum Student Loan Payment	-$800
Groceries & Restaurants	-$450
Truck Note	-$400
Gas & Car Insurance	-$500
Cell Phones, TV & Internet	-$200
Leftover Money	**$2000**

The old saying goes, "when you make more money, you spend more money". This was certainly true for us as you can see from the difference just two years made in our monthly spending habits. All in all, we were still doing fantastic. I didn't know anyone that had a $2000 cushion in their monthly expenses. Our dual incomes were amazing, and they easily afforded us the big, new, expensive house we always wanted.

If you haven't guessed it yet, this $2000 dollar "cushion" way of thinking is exactly what got us in trouble. Yes, it was true we could afford almost anything we wanted in this monthly scheme. Two thousand dollars is a lot of money, but this whole scheme only worked as long as we maintained our income from our jobs. Not having ANY longer-term plans outside of doing everything we could to fight to maintain our jobs was the heart of the issue looking back.

This "cushion" mind set within a monthly income stream is the exact definition of "living paycheck to paycheck". Things work out great month to month as long as our paychecks came in month after month. We always carried about $10K in our savings account at this point, but as you can see, that would have only let us survive for about 2 months if we lost our incomes. You will see how thinking about our money this way got us in trouble.

During 2015, something else fortunate did occur for us as well. I had bought my truck in 2011 and had always paid a little extra per month just to round up the truck note to $400. As a result, we ended up paying off my truck in 2015 because it was on a 5-year payment plan. We only had about $2-3K left to pay it off by that point. So, we did.

Unfortunately, we turned right around that same year and traded in Steph's paid off truck for a brand-new Dodge Durango. Her truck had been getting older by that point (about 150K miles) so we figured it was a good time to take on another car payment because we had just paid mine off. So, paying off my truck during this time didn't actually help us much as far as our monthly budget was concerned. We basically stayed right where we were after making this car swap.

Regardless of this car decision we made, we still had about $2K in leftover money per month after all bills were paid. So, what did we do with that? We actually did something smart! We started paying aggressively on our student loans. Our first small school loan we paid off was $1500 that I had taken out years back. It had a fifty dollar minimum payment. Steph and I discussed it, and agreed it seemed like a good idea to just knock that one out quickly because it was low hanging fruit. And we did. The following month, we got a congratulations letter from whatever lender, thanking us for paying it off. Just like that, within one month in 2015, we decreased our monthly minimum student loan payments from $800 to $750 per month. And more importantly, we INCREASED our leftover money from $2000 to $2050 per month. I can't stress enough that the increase of fifty dollars to our monthly leftover is the key thought here.

We continued in this manner for the rest of 2015 and all of 2016 chunking most of our leftover money to school loans. There were definitely speed bumps along the way that stopped us from contributing all of our leftover money towards student loans every single month. Examples would be needing new truck tires after I could no longer pass a vehicle inspection. We spent almost $3K on a billiards table that I had always wanted. We had to furnish our house with new furniture because we didn't have any furniture coming from a small apartment. And we made some backyard improvements to our new house by having a new concrete pad poured along with a cedar pergola built which totaled $6K. Besides the truck tires, most of these things were things we wanted, and not things we needed. We were making decent progress on our school loans during these years, but we weren't aggressively attacking them. We were trying to balance our lives with things we wanted versus things we knew were good for us. It was a kind of semi "You Only Live Once" (YOLO) attitude.

Looking back now, half diligence towards paying student loans, and half YOLO mind set was us trying to balance our lives in the best way we knew how. Life was good for us, and we were living it how we wanted to. We didn't have any thought towards an exterior factor invading our lives and wrecking the life we built. We had this magnificent income, so how would it ever change other than go up slowly as the years passed? Those paychecks kept rolling in month after month and year after year. They would never stop it seemed. What reason was there to live our lives with the expectation that 7700 dollars WASN'T going to hit our bank account each month? In 2015, that answer did not have a reason. In 2016 things changed, and that answer absolutely DID have reason.

In 2016, the price of oil dropped steadily and considerably due to an oversupply of oil to the world in general. I had now been working for an oil company for almost three years and the consequences of the price of oil dropping were extreme at my workplace in 2016 and 2017. I had never been through a down cycle of oil prices during my working career. For a kid who committed himself in the first grade to his schoolwork, finished college with flying colors, and found the dream job he had always wanted making more money than he thought possible; the price of oil tanking was like fear injected into my veins.

The fear wasn't immediate or life threatening in any way. However, it was like a constant weight that slowly got heavier on my shoulders month after month. It became unbelievably heavy in the last quarter of 2016. It was clear through company management, whisperings, cooler talks, and gossip that people were going to get laid off.

I truly didn't believe anything was actually going to happen. Nothing had ever happened before. Why would it happen now? I somewhat blew it off in my mind convincing myself that getting laid off could never happen to me. I was a good employee. I put all my efforts into the tasks assigned to me every time. As I said, I was grateful to my employer for my job, my salary, and for the life it afforded my wife and I. My effort level at work exemplified that. Of course, I was safe.

I worked in a group of about fifteen people all of whom did a myriad of things from supply chain, engineering, drafting, and management. One fine October morning at 9 AM, two engineers were let go from my company to my shock and disbelief. Worse than that, I had come to find out from my co-workers who worked in other buildings that they had seen similar numbers of people leave their respective groups. By the end of the day, it was clear that about 10% of the Houston based workforce of my company had been let go from their positions. It was a bad day at work, but at least I had been spared.

I came home that night with my mind a complete mess. I had texted Steph to tell her what happened that morning already. That day was the start of my mind shifting to a new way of thinking. I had always thought I could work for my company forever if I wanted to. They had given me so much. Why would I not return the favor for the life my company allowed me to have? I always thought I would be that guy walking across a stage 30 years later, shaking the hand of my

CEO, who would hand me my 30-year plaque of service to my company. I was perfectly content to be that guy.

However, letting two people go unexpectedly without warning, who had families at home, completely burst that bubble of me shaking the CEO's hand one day. It could have been me that day, coming home to my wife at 10AM explaining how I had just got laid off from my job. I had worked so hard my whole life, FROM THE FIRST GRADE, to ensure that I had financial stability in my life. And just like that, my supposed stability could have been over that day without any warning.

I was pissed. I was angry. Most of all, I was scared. Luckily, today had not been my day. But you can bet it felt like I had just been punched in the mouth. So, what do you do when you get punched in the mouth? You simply get back up and keep moving forward. This is what 80% of my co-workers did around me. They kept on working, pretending nothing had happened, but still acknowledged that it sucked if the topic came up in conversation. These people were smart. They found a way to push down any anxiety they may feel from losing their co-workers despite knowing they could be next. They buried themselves in their work and tried to carry on the day to day.

Being smart wasn't good enough for me, however. Over the course of the next number of months, I recognized that about 20% of the people I worked with did not fall into this "smart" category. These people had all different reactions ranging from extreme bitterness towards our employer, to needing to take more paid time off, to working extremely long hours to finish major projects to ensure they were successful. A small handful of people I knew simply decided to resign on their own within the next number of months. These different reactions were shocking to me. I didn't know how to classify these people other than mysteries. The psychology of what drives people to do what they do is a fascinating subject in my opinion. This lay-off event at my company was a spectacle to watch for these reasons. I understood why 80% of the people I knew put their head down and went back to work. I didn't understand the reactions from the other 20%, however. All I knew was what I saw happening around me, and what I observed in myself. I willingly joined the smart, 80% of people in my office. I desperately needed a way to cope with the stress of knowing that I could be next.

However, that was my attitude at work and work only. At home, I slowly became someone different. Home was a place that provided a stress-free environment, but now, that was no longer the case. I knew at any moment we may not be able to afford our stress-free environment if I got let go. There would be no peace at home for me or Steph if we couldn't afford the mortgage! Something had to change. For Steph and I, that change started with us. We recognized that we needed to do something. So we did!

I want to break down our reality at this point in terms of monthly budget numbers. Numbers don't lie, so how would our monthly budget be affected if I had been let go in 2016? Losing my job would have cut about $4100 out of our monthly income, leaving us with about $3600 per month. The house note alone was $2850, so add in the basic utilities and it was about $3350 per month. That left us almost no room to eat or put gas in the car! The reality of our situation was on the cliff's edge, and we had walked ourselves right up to that cliff.

After a few weeks of discussion, Steph and I put our brand-new home on the market after living in it for just over two years. We used a realtor who listed it for $328K, $23K over what we had paid for it. Something had to change in our lives. The anxiety of not knowing if my employer would allow me to stay working for them the next day was too much. At work, I pretended everything was fine and pushed my anxiety down with the daily routine. Having our house listed on the market was relieving. It felt good knowing we were doing something towards putting our fate back in our own hands if we could get it to sell!

The Lesson

During 2015 and 2016, it was enlightening to realize the things we actually had control of in our lives. The price of oil and my company's response to that was something that we had absolutely no control over. We did, however, have control of the place we lived, the management of our monthly budget, and our relationship with each other. I know that sounds simple, but sometimes you don't really know what you have until someone threatens to take it away. Our big new house that we loved very much was in jeopardy, but we weren't going to fight to keep it if I lost my job. We knew that would be financial suicide.

Only two years before we had been very happy together in our little two-bedroom apartment. We both understood back then that home is defined as the place where you make it, and the place where your other person is. Whether that's in a two-bedroom apartment, a 5000 square foot mansion, or a car under the highway. We had each other, and while it hurt to let the house go, we could make a new home anywhere we needed to. As we have gotten older, our marriage and confidence have grown exponentially with this idea. I can't help but feel that these ideas are somehow tied into why married people live longer than single people statistically. I have no proof of this, but it definitely feels like a piece to that puzzle.

Chapter 8: Downsizing Life

In early 2017, we sold our house for $316K after all was settled. The housing market was not busting at the seams for a suburban area Houston home at the time, especially one in this price range. This was a fair price for the house, and we were anxious to get it sold. It ended up sitting on the market for 4-5 months before an offer came along, and that was after we reduced the price one time after about 2-3 months.

I feel like I can hear your questions jumping out at me. Why did you sell that house for $316K when you bought it for $305K only a few years ago? A home seller will pay an estimated 6% at closing in realtor fees alone. Six percent of $316K is roughly $19K due at closing for realtor fees. If this is something you thought about, then you are right. However, we did negotiate down our realtor's fees by about $5K which helped the situation greatly. We did have to agree to buy a new home with that realtor, which we were fine with, but that was part of the negotiation.

So, we ended owing about $17K in total closing costs for the sale of that house. We owed about $285K on the mortgage

55

because we had put 5% down when we bought it, and we had paid the principal down slightly over the last two years. Therefore, we walked away with a check from the title company for about $14K after the whole transaction was complete ($316K - $17K - $285K = $14K).

We quickly turned around and found an older home to buy closer to Steph's work for $238K. We used the $14K we got from the sale of our home and bought it on a 30-year conventional loan with 5% down (~$12K). After moving expenses, we basically broke even on the entire transaction. The way we thought about the entire situation was that we almost got to live for free in our big, new house for 2 years. This isn't quite accurate, as the entire transaction did cost us some money. However, it wasn't money that we felt any immediate pain from. At the end of the day, it felt good to simply remove that mortgage payment from our lives.

We already knew we had to downsize our life. To us that meant cutting down our monthly budget as much as possible. By moving closer to Steph's work, we were saving money on gas for her because we were anticipating I might get laid off from my job any day. On top of this, the home we bought was over $75K cheaper than the one we had just sold. In addition, interest rates had declined by almost a full percentage point in between 2014 and 2017. Also, the area we chose had a significantly reduced property tax rate by about .5% over where we lived before. Combining all of this, the result was phenomenal! By the spring of 2017, our finances settled down and we cut $1000 out of our monthly expenses. All of this was due to our new mortgage payment of only $1800 per month. Including utilities and yearly HOA, our house expenses were right at $2200 per month.

It was now possible for us to survive! The relief we felt after moving was crazy! We now had a way to survive even if we lost my income. While we wouldn't be able to completely live off Steph's income; our small $10K savings coupled with her income was enough to buy us much more time when I lost my job. Here is a breakdown of our monthly budget in the spring of 2017:

Monthly Expenses – Spring of 2017	
Monthly Paychecks	$7700
Mortgage	-$1800
Utilities + HOA	-$400
Minimum Student Loan Payment	-$650
Groceries & Restaurants	-$450
Steph's Car Note	-$400
Gas & Car Insurance	-$500
Cell Phones, TV & Internet	-$200
Leftover Money	**$3300**

Downsizing had a dramatic effect on our mental attitude towards money. It had a huge effect on how we thought about our student loans in particular because we knew we could do some real damage to them! To now have $3300 in leftover money per month; it was astounding so much of our income was freed up by this house move! I take for granted how much this was at the time, but my fear of being let go from my job completely overshadowed what we had accomplished in our monthly budget. Our plan was to take full advantage of the time I had left with my current employer, and we totally did that!

Shortly after our move to this less expensive house, a few positive and negative things took place during the rest of 2017. The most positive of which was that Steph was beginning to really stand out at her job. Opportunities began to present themselves to her because she was also a good employee that cared about her job and worked hard every day. She received an award for employee of the year at her hospital and she had taken a new position as an admissions and discharge nurse towards the end of 2016 instead of the bedside nurse she had been previously. She got a small pay bump, but the job was something different for her, which was what she was craving.

Also during 2017, Steph and I began building our handyman skills! We began acquiring tools slowly in 2017 because our house was old and needed some remodel efforts. We decided to attempt small projects that only required minimum plumbing, painting, and tiling skills. Many of which we learned on YouTube! During our weekends off we found ourselves knee deep in all kinds of flooring and painting projects. By the end of 2019 we had almost totally redone our house with own hands. Ill admit that our skills were sub-par on some of our projects. But as we did it more, we got better at everything we did. Remodeling turned into something that we both enjoyed doing together, despite my fears at work.

By the end of 2017, my job was mentally taking a toll on me. Another layoff occurred in the summer of 2017 which cut an additional 10% off the workforce at my company. Two more people were forced to leave the group I was working in, but somehow, I was not included once again. I made it through two major layoffs at my company and it really started messing with my mind. I wasn't the only one though. One of the best ways to destroy a company's culture is to randomly let go of your employees. Everyone that I now worked with had made it through two layoffs, which was both good and bad because the gossip around the office hinted that layoffs would continue into 2018. While I now knew I could handle being let go financially, I started to wonder how my co-worker's lives had been affected by layoffs over the last year. During this time, my co-workers including myself, began to more freely talk about how everything was affecting us. We shared our anger, frustration, and simply our fears of not knowing whom would be next. It was not a healthy working situation by any means.

In addition to more layoffs, I now had an extreme commute to work. I spent a little less than 2 hours in the car each day. 1 hour there, and 1 hour back since we had moved closer to Steph's work. It was good that I was still employed, but I didn't actually think I would survive a second layoff. Our gas bill and my sanity with such a long commute really took a toll on my mental health from 2017 into 2019.

The vicious cycle of a daily commute was one of the more difficult problems that I hadn't anticipated while working a job that paid me so much. While I did have the weekends free to myself, I dreaded the coming Monday every time 6:00 PM Sunday would roll around. It meant another work week that I had to fight through just to get up at 5:00 AM, get to work, and make it home in time for dinner. The constant cycle of 5:00 AM wake up, to work by 6:30, deal with the stress of a workday, and leave by 3:30-4PM to make it home to spend only 4 waking hours at home was terrible. I began to contemplate sleeping at work one day a week because that seemed like a better use of my time than spending so much time commuting. I know what the older folks would say to this, because my dad would have given me the same advice if he had still been around. "Suck it up son! This is work. This is what it means to grow up, take care of your family, and put food on the table!"

Unless you have been caught in this work cycle for many years, it's hard for me to describe the mental deterioration that one slowly experiences over a period of time. Dealing with this for one year, is possible for anyone if you have to do it. Dealing with it for two years is still possible, but it begins to eat away at your soul because you feel as if your life has lost some of its meaning. It eats all the hope you have for your life, all your dreams, because you feel as if your stuck getting up each morning only to spend 4 hours at home in the evening just to pay the bills. It's a feeling of hopelessness.

The ironic thing about this is that I saw my mother go through this as a child. When I saw it then, I used it as inspiration to do well in school. I flipped it in a positive manner for me. I did not want to end up with the hopelessness that my mother felt back then. Yet here I was! Albeit a different set of circumstances, but the core feeling of hopelessness was the same. I was making much more money than she ever had, yet I was fighting the same feelings I had seen in her. I had put myself here! Into the very thing I was trying to avoid! This more than anything was a major lightbulb moment in my life during this time. I couldn't believe I had willingly walked into this nonsense. Something had to change. You can bet I was going to find a way out of this!

The Lesson

Downsizing our life had a tremendous effect on our livelihood. While such a decision is not ideal, it felt like one of the only choices we had at the time. The alternative was to do nothing and hope I kept my job, but it's hard to communicate my experiences to you from my workplace. I truly believed I could be let go at any moment based on the information I had. No one wants to move into a smaller, less expensive house. You generally hope as your life goes on that you step UP in house once or twice in your lifetime whether it be as your family grows, or you make more money. But we didn't do that. Those weren't the cards dealt to Steph and I, so we had to play our hand the best way we could.

Steph's income in late 2017 was right around $3600-3700 per month. We were only a few hundred dollars away from her income being all of our leftover money per month. It was highly encouraging in so many ways. If you ever have the opportunity to downsize your life in a dramatic way in order to increase your monthly income by 15-20% or more, I highly encourage it. To us, it was like finding free money and it didn't affect our lifestyle one bit. Us downsizing allowed us to see much more clearly what we needed to do with our finances. We were trying to prepare for the day I might be let go, while simultaneously looking for ways to increase our leftover monthly budget now that we had drastically increased it. We did it once, why couldn't we do it again? We set our sights on the only other major thing that had been bogging us down since finishing college. Student loans!

Chapter 9: Paid off Student Loans!

B y the early spring of 2017, we had a little over $55K in student loans still left to pay. We had made some progress over the last three years paying off about $8K per year since 2014. We could have done more during this time, but as I said, we had been balancing our lifestyle in the best way we knew how by buying things we wanted while simultaneously paying our student loans. We started with a grand total of $80K back in 2013 and had only reduced our monthly payments slightly by this point. I want to note a few things regarding our approach towards paying our student loans.

First, we never missed one minimum payment on any of these student loans. Whether the minimum was $30 or $200 we always prioritized paying the minimums while simultaneously targeting our leftover income towards ONE of the loans until it was gone. Our goal was to free up our monthly expenses, NOT to pay off the entire school loan debt (although obviously happened as we paid each one down). We were trying to survive in case I lost my job.

Second, we never got caught up in any nonsense with interest payments stacking up on themselves. Sometimes people take out certain types of loans for school that accumulate interest while they are in school and during any grace/forbearance periods. None of our loans were this type. They were very straight forward where each minimum payment did pay a small amount towards the principal owed. Even making minimum payments did slightly lower our principal balances each month despite how big or small that minimum payment was.

Lastly, we did something smart during this time that really helped us make a final push at knocking out our student loans. Steph had a bunch of little loans (8-10 of them) that had principals of anywhere from $500 to $4000. They each had higher than average interest rates too, ranging from 7-9% (a good average interest rate during this time period was anything from 3-6%). We had been researching debt consolidation companies for the last few months but had yet to move forward on anything until this point. It seemed like a good idea to go ahead and lower the interest rate on Steph's loans if we could accomplish it.

Armed with a plan to slowly pay off our student loans within the next 2 years, we went ahead and consolidated all of Steph's little loans into one big loan totaling about $25K with an adjustable interest rate of 3%. The adjustable rate stayed locked at 3% for one year, and then it was subject to adjustment after that 12-month period. While the adjustable interest rate scared us a little, we made a plan to combat it. That 12-month fixed period at 3% was more than enough time for us to knock out the remaining $30K that we weren't consolidating using our newly found monthly leftover money ($3300 X 12 = $39,600) Knowing this, we went for it! We consolidated Steph's high interest rate loans down to 3% and locked them there for one year. We kept making the minimum payment on this loan but focused intensely on paying off all other student loans with higher interest rates.

By the beginning of 2018, we had done it! We stayed highly focused on using our leftover money per month to crack down on the non-consolidated $30K in student loans we had. I wish I could tell you it was difficult or something, but it wasn't. We didn't have any major life events or disasters during this time period that caused us to have to deviate from this plan. We both went to work, sucked it up, made that money every month, and quickly got into a habit of paying more than $3000 per month on our student loans. Once the habit of paying that much per month was formed, it became easier to let that money go. We weren't happy about it, but we had made a goal together and we were going to achieve it. Just like a few years earlier when we were saving all of Steph's income in order to save for a down payment on a home. We applied the same principle here. However, instead of it all going into our bank account, it went to the student loan people.

We were HIGHLY encouraged with our progress in early 2018. We had paid back $55K in student loans since we graduated in 2013! It was truly an astounding amount of money to us. All we had left was the last $25K consolidated loan. These loan people had already sent us a letter informing us that they were increasing our interest rate by a quarter of a percent in March of 2018. We had anticipated this might happen, but now we had the ability to go full throttle at this last $25K. Because we had paid off all our other school loans, we had freed up an additional $500 per month that we could apply to this loan. At minimum we paid $3500 per month on this consolidated loan in a final push effort to finish it!

The only hiccup we had in our plan was that we underestimated how quickly the new adjustable interest rate would increase. In the summer of 2018, this company bumped our interest rate to 3.75% up from 3 where it started. However, once we got the loan balance below $10K, they stopped increasing it. By that point it didn't really matter what the interest rate was any way. The balance was decreasing so fast that our interest payments were almost nothing, especially after the balance was under $10K.

In the fall of 2018, something magical happened. I had never heard of anyone paying off their student loans in my life; not of people I knew, friends or family of any kind. It had always seemed like student loans were something people dealt with for their entire lives. Like it was some kind of price to pay for the privilege of going to college, because what other way was there? The cost of college is (and was back then) so high, that no normal person could afford it without help. Student loans were just something you lived with as a consequence of going to college. Or so I thought.

By September of 2018, Steph and I had paid EIGHTY THOUSAND DOLLARS back to a handful of student loan companies over the course of 5 years. I'll say it again, so that maybe it sinks in. WE PAID OFF OUR STUDENT LOANS! It was something I didn't think was possible! The weight of a debt totaling $80K was a crazy amount of money to me. My parents each only made $40K on average for a whole year! How was it possible to pay such a large sum back? I hope the answer is clear to you now. It took over 5 years of making a point to pay extra on these loans. It took five years of refraining from buying other things we wanted in order to prioritize accomplishing a goal we both wanted.

My hope is that this story provides you with a small piece of encouragement to know that IT IS possible to pay off your student loans. I didn't think it was possible when we started. Yet I stand on the other side of them now without them in my life. The biggest win for the rest of our lives is that we freed up $800 of our monthly income to go towards ANYTHING else other than student loans. That money was free to go into a savings account, or an investment account, or the mortgage, or a vacation, or even be blown in Vegas! ANYTHING we chose to do with this extra $800 per month felt like a better plan than giving it to the student loan people any longer. IT IS AN AWESOME FEELING! It's one I hope you get to experience in your life because there are some experiences worth feeling before you die. To me, paying off this large debt was one of them. It finally felt like we had crossed the threshold for survival even if I lost my job now. THAT was a huge weight lifted off our shoulders.

As big of a win this was in our lives, 2018 still wasn't a good year to be working for an oil company. A few months before we paid off our student loans, another round of layoffs occurred at my company. This time, it more directly affected me more than the previous two. This time, my direct manager was let go without warning. She was one of the better managers during my time at this company, but that was not enough to keep her around. I can remember her not being shocked by this decision the day it happened. In fact, it was like she knew it was going to occur in the weeks leading up to it. However, I did not take her departure well. I was NOT prepared for her to leave so suddenly. The mental toll of surviving three rounds of layoffs with my employer was a sort of breaking point for me. Couple this with a commute I despised which I had been making for a little over a year now. My mind went to a route I did not expect.

Do you remember me joining the "smart" people at my company who simply went back to work with their heads down after the first layoffs in 2016? Yeah, I was no longer joining those people. I understood better about the 20% of my co-workers whom I had classified as mysteries. I had not understood their reactions back then, but I understood them now.

I was no longer fearful of being let go from my company. That fear had been replaced with anger, frustration, and spite towards my employer. I understood that my company wasn't doing well and that something needed to be done, but I hated them for not trying harder to find creative ways to keep more employees employed. Strangely enough, letting go of my fear of being let go made me a better performing employee. I now made daily decisions with little regard for the consequences of these decisions because if my employer didn't care enough to make an attempt to value there employees, why should I care about the company's success?

My new attitude actually landed me a semi-promotion (more work, same pay) leading the engineering of a 12-million-dollar project with a major longstanding account. (Don't forget, my promotion was NOT a result of my hard work, or my new attitude towards my job. There were also over 30% fewer employees in my office now, so there were far fewer choices of people left to lead existing projects). While I was able to make decisions quickly and often make them in sound judgement, I secretly hoped I would screw it up somehow. While it turned out I was decently good at my new role, the reasoning in which I was good at it was a horribly negative emotion in my heart. As I helped steer my project ahead of schedule and under budget, I struggled to contain the negative disposition that I felt towards my employer.

It was a strange time in my life! I was succeeding at home in our personal finances and succeeding with flying colors on my first major project at work yet, I was dealing with extreme resentment towards my company despite the fact the things were going very well for me. I was a mess. It felt like Steph and I had accomplished so much in the last few years. We set goals, kept to them, and made things happen. We largely felt that our destinies resided in our own hands. We had built up our confidence both in each other and in what we could accomplish. So, what was next?

The Lesson

Feeling the accomplishment of achieving a major financial milestone in our lives was exhilarating. Not only had we figured out how to survive if one of us lost our job, we built up our confidence in each other to believe that we could tackle anything. Nothing compares to working hard for a long period of time and accomplishing a major goal that you set many years ago. The act of achieving something in this manner is very different than the "want it now" attitude that our society seeks to obtain around every corner. Yes, it's possible to win the lottery or inherit a bunch of money, but they are not probable for the vast majority of us. Statistically, you have a better chance of being struck by lighting. It's just not worth any mental thought to spend time hoping for this to happen to you. Setting goals of any kind, both small and large, are a major key to becoming a millionaire. It took us 5 years to pay back $80K. That is no small amount of time and not something that happened over night. It took diligence, patience, and tenacity to accomplish it. Anyone can do it; you just have to want it bad enough. In our case, the threat of me losing my job was enough to fuel us to accomplish it and get it done.

Chapter 10: Emergence

B etween the spring of 2017 and the fall of 2018, our monthly expenses took a wild swing in a wonderful direction thanks to paying off our school loans. The breakdown is as follows. I will note our incomes did both slightly increase during this time due to the new role Steph had started as well as yearly raises that most employers provide. Even my company decided to give annual raises despite letting go of 10% of their workforce in 2018. It was just another detail that confused me regarding letting so many people go yet bumping everyone's pay up by an average of 3%.

Monthly Expenses – Fall of 2018	
Monthly Paychecks	$8300
Mortgage	-$1800
Utilities + HOA	-$400
Minimum Student Loan Payment	-$0!
Groceries & Restaurants	-$450
Steph's Car Note	-$400
Gas & Car Insurance	-$500
Cell Phones, TV & Internet	-$200
Leftover Money	**$4550**

As I said before, the true power in us paying off our school loans wasn't that we paid off the debt. It was that we freed up $800 per month to now add to our leftover money! Can you even imagine having over $4500 per month in extra money that you don't have to pay bills with? To this day, I still have a hard time comprehending this. It was just so much money! We had so much power to spend our money how we wanted now. It was crazy.

It wasn't all kittens and rainbows. Obviously, we were still fearful of me losing my job. The fall of 2018 was the tipping point where we would be able to pay all our bills on Steph's income alone if the worst did happen. We definitely crossed a major threshold at that time in our lives. The real question was what now? What would you do in our situation with this much extra monthly income, but also knowing the party could be over tomorrow?

Our answer was straight forward. As I said, I was no longer fearful of losing my job, but I was also comforted by our newfound success of no longer NEEDING my job. We had found a rhythm of paying back our student loans over the last two years, so we applied that rhythm to the last remaining target in our monthly budget that we knew was achievable. We targeted Steph's car note. It seemed like a good idea. Why not provide a little cushion for ourselves instead of just trying to squeak by if I didn't have a job tomorrow? So that's what we did.

By early 2019, we had Steph's car completely paid for. We had about $20K left on the note to pay off back then. And we knocked that thing out fast! Paying over $4K per month on anything would make a serious dent in it. But we took this car note down in closer to four months rather than five. We used our newfound rhythm and attacked it like you wouldn't believe. Any extra money we "found" in our budget during that time went towards the car, even if it was only fifty bucks. At minimum we committed to pay $4K per month on it, but in reality, we found a way to pay closer to $5K per month to get it done.

Here's an update of update our monthly expenses during this time. It was crazy, that's all I can say.

Monthly Expenses – Early 2019	
Monthly Paychecks	$8300
Mortgage	-$1800
Utilities + HOA	-$400
Minimum Student Loan Payment	-$0!
Groceries & Restaurants	-$450
Steph's Car Note	-$0!
Gas & Car Insurance	-$500
Cell Phones, TV & Internet	-$200
Leftover Money	**$4950**

Putting in just 4 more months of paying Steph's car down got us knocking on the door of having $5K per month in additional income that we didn't need. I can't stress to you enough how these numbers hurt my head sometimes. Neither of our single mother households growing up had such a thing. We would have been lucky just to have our mothers bring in $5K per month to cover living expenses when we were young. Now, to have it be EXTRA income is something I will always have trouble wrapping my mind around.

I'll ask you again, what would you do now if you had an extra $5K coming in over your monthly living expenses? Back then, we didn't have an answer for you. It was only after this point that I started reading financial books and educating myself in the ways that people become wealthy. Knowing what I know now, there are a plethora of things someone can do if you find yourself in a situation like this. We could have increased our retirement percentages withheld at our jobs, or opened an investment account, or saved some in the bank, or opened a 529 plan for ourselves and our future children or paid down the mortgage. It even would have been okay for us to blow an entire $5-10K on just a celebration vacation for ourselves! The list goes on and on! This list of good ideas is almost limitless when you get to this point because as long as you don't go crazy, YOU CAN ACTUALLY AFFORD TO DO WHAT YOU WANT!

I'd like to tell you we did something nuts and blew $10K in Vegas or something. But we didn't. We were boring, but also realistic because we knew our success may not last. All we did was save the extra money. We saved about $5K per month after that to build up our savings account. We had always kept somewhere between $10-15K in there at this point. By the summer of 2019 we had well over $40K in our bank account. We were now fully prepared in every way for me to lose my job. Armed with almost a full year's worth of living expenses in our savings account, all that was left was for me to actually get the boot!

While all of this financial security is going on in our home lives, my work life was at a breaking point in my mind. Have you ever worked with a co-worker who just seems bitter about being at work every day? They are generally a negative person and can sometimes be very vocal, even in front of management, about how they feel about certain situations. I was that guy. I was that guy you hate! Sorry about that. My sincere apologies if you are reading this and I ever offended you with my snide remarks and negative point of view on life. The crazy thing is the project I was leading during this time was doing wonderfully well. I was working my ass off to make sure it was running smoothly, but I just had a horribly bad attitude towards my employer anytime I wasn't in front of the customer. I'm telling you; it was a strange situation. I even got a $500 Visa gift card at one point as a thank you from my boss for doing so well. My brain was not computing correctly anymore.

After we got Steph's car paid off in early 2019, I can clearly remember that my horrible, negative attitude started to come home with me much more. Having one bad day at work every once in a while is totally fine, especially when you can vent to your spouse. But I was coming home almost every day with negative things to say about my company and my project. Yet, I threw down $500 dollar gift cards on the dinner table. Steph understood I wasn't doing well. After a couple years of her seeing my attitude slowly escalate, she fully embraced that I needed a change in my life. She wanted to see me happier.

The Lesson

The act of getting into a rhythm to tackle debt is probably one of the most important lessons for becoming a millionaire. Debt that carries high interest rates or eats a large portion of your monthly income are things that millionaires typically don't have. Millionaires are not made through credit card rewards or by suing the guy who bumped you from behind in a small fender bender. If you are a millionaire from these things, then you will not be a millionaire for much longer. People who are wealthy with net worth's in the multimillion-dollar range have built positive money habits over a long period of time to help them achieve their status. Paying off debt owed to other people is one such positive habit.

By utilizing the funds you have available to you every month, you can form a plan to slowly work your way out of debt. By slowly increasing your leftover money per month, by targeting and paying down debt, you can slowly roll that ball down the hill. The ball will gain momentum as you pay off smaller debts first and then you can apply those minimum payments to larger debts. The process can be done by anyone. You simply have to have the will to do it. Stephanie and I would finish paying something off, and then roll that extra money per month into the next debt we targeted to pay. That's the secret.

What's fascinating after you accomplish paying off your consumer debts, school loans, cars, personal loans, and all debt besides real estate mortgages, your mind begins to view the world differently. It's a very positive feeling. It's a feeling that makes you believe you can tackle the world. It builds your self-confidence to the point where you can begin to think of creative ways to help your family, friends, and the people in your community. You are not a burden to yourself any longer because you are now able to provide for yourself with ease. It frees up your mind to focus on other activities that you could never consider before because you were once bogged down by the weight of others whom you owed things to.

My father worked a job for over 40 years of his life before he passed away. I can tell you that he did not experience what

I'm talking about here. He was always weighed down by car payments, car repairs, child support, and his addictions. There are millions of people living now who do not believe they can ever experience what I've described. There are many millions more who have died that missed their chance to experience it. I am sad for these people. They tried to fight against the hopelessness that this culture brings into our lives, but eventually succumbed to it and lost that fight. You must never give up, and you must find a reason for yourself to exit the hopelessness that you might be in. Otherwise, you will be stuck there for your entire life. The physical workout the guy next to you does every morning doesn't change YOUR physical appearance in anyway. The same is true of your finances. Only you can change it.

Lastly, one small tool I started for Steph and I in 2019 was something that was very helpful to me personally. I started tracking our total net worth and committed to updating it at least four times a year. I continue it to this day. It's a basic file I built in Excel that lists all our debts and assets. In addition to this, I make small notes about what happened each quarter that made the number change either up or down. For example, mortgage pay downs, stock market trends, work bonuses, debt pay downs etc. For some people it is helpful to track their progress in this way. My wife is not one of them, but I certainly am. Seeing progress being made in this manner keeps me motivated and diligent. I encourage you to start doing this for yourself. It will highlight whether you are on an uptrend or downtrend after three full quarters. Seeing your net worth trend may help you to get focused towards becoming a millionaire.

Chapter 11: New Mind, New Opportunity & Possums

In late 2018, a new opportunity presented itself to us in a way that we did not expect. We had paid off our student loans and were very close to finishing paying off Steph's car. A large portion of our income was free at this point, so we had a very different point of view about money compared to just about all our family members. Which for us, being 27 and 28 years old was new for the first time. The following opportunity had both positive and negative financial decisions made by us during this time. I'll address the whole story in the hope that you don't make the same mistake, while also paying attention to the intelligent aspect of the situation that became of all this. This story is also a wonderful example of how all business deals can shape the world positively for everyone involved.

Steph's grandmother has lived in the Bryan/College Station area for more than 40 years. She raised five children there and worked for Texas A&M University for much of that time. She is an awesome lady that has seen A LOT and is 80 years old now. She has lived by herself for the last 20 years and works hard to maintain her independence. She enjoys when her children and grandchildren come to visit like most grandmothers do. At the same time, it's always been clear to me that she is happy when visiting time is over. Whether that be from her personal exhaustion throughout a day or from the relief she feels to live a simple life in her own place, I can't be sure. I do know she is an awesome lady to have dinner with from time to time.

Everything started when a family member discovered that possums had taken up residence inside grandma's home! Somehow, they had chewed through the floorboards of her pier and beam house and taken up lodging inside the bottom of her couch. I can remember her telling me a story of when she opened her dishwasher one morning and found a fully grown possum inside! Among other small stories of her pantry being raided and such, one major event about the possums really set things in motion.

Possums are mostly active at night, so they were scavenging through the inside of her house while she slept. Grandma had a habit of turning up her TV at night as she fell asleep and not wearing her hearing aids (even though she needed them). This led to a living situation that was not favorable on any account. One night, grandma woke to the sound of claws scratching against the top of the headboard where she slept. She was promptly scared and hissed at by an adult possum trying to walk across the top of her bed! We heard a secondhand account of this event from Steph's mother and wondered what grandma was going to do about this situation. I mean, you can't make this stuff up! This really happened!

Afterwards, we realized grandma's house was not in the best shape. The possums were only the tip of the iceberg. The house had a significant foundation issue and some other more minor problems. At the time, her house issues weren't something we knew how to fix or even begin to repair. We knew grandma didn't have the money for a significant foundation repair, so Steph and I discussed a plan to try and help her grandma in a major way.

In the short term, different family members in the area helped with slowly catching the possums in the house and relocating them as they were caught. It turned out an entire family of possums had grown up underneath her house the previous year! I can't tell you how many there were in total, but I remember it being more than three adults for sure. With the possum problem temporarily under control, we formed a plan with grandma to sell her house as it was and help her move into a new house that Steph and I would buy for her.

Grandma's retirement income back then wasn't enough to qualify her for a loan for anything more than the type of house she lived in currently. On top of this, the Bryan/College Station area is a particularly hot real estate market at all times of the year. There are a ton of students renting all year as well as a large, retired community. The bottom line is any home for sale under $150K (in 2018) doesn't last long on the market. Grandma's house was solidly in this range in the condition it was in. So, we went ahead and listed her house on the market with an agreement that Steph and I would buy a second home for her to live in. Due to the fact that I still had my job at this time, Steph and I easily qualified for a loan on a second home as long as we put 20% down on something around the $200K price range

Our arrangement with grandma was that she agreed to roll the equity she had from the sale of her current home into the new home, which ended up being about $20K. Steph and I would contribute an additional $20K into the down payment for a total of $40K. Our interest rate would be a little higher on this loan compared to a normal primary residence loan (the interest rate was right at 4.25%), but this yielded a mortgage payment of $1300 per month on a $200K priced home. We agreed to split the mortgage payment with grandma, but she would take care of paying all the utilities. At this point we had a serious talk about grandma's monthly income and figured out that she could afford this without too much trouble. We were actually reducing her housing expenses slightly by doing this.

So, with a little bit of difficulty navigating the college station housing market, we did eventually sell grandma's house and find a new place for her with a wonderful local realtor. Now that you have the basic idea of how we entered this deal with grandma, I want to fully explain all the advantages this arrangement created for everyone. For grandma, she no longer deals with possums or even the possibility of possums showing up at her house. She lives in a house that is between $50-80K more expensive than she can afford on her sole income. She pays below market rent by about 50%. Her housing costs are lower overall than when she owned her own home because Steph and I agreed to take care of any home repairs that arise in the future. This also means that she has more freedom in her monthly budget to do as she pleases. Most importantly, grandma maintains her ability to live independently while still having a place for her children and grandchildren to visit her when they want.

For Steph and I, this arrangement lets us capture the gains from all the longer term benefits of owning a home. We are younger, so these things appeal to us more than they do to grandma. Realistically, grandma knows that she has somewhere between 10-20 years left of her life. While this can be a difficult subject to address personally as a family, Steph's grandma has never had an issue with discussing this. She actually jokes to us that she doesn't want to live 20 more years! As I said, she is an awesome lady. Regardless of this tough aging discussion, Steph and I will catch the market appreciation of this home over the next 10-20 years while grandma is still with us. On top of that, we will benefit from the principal pay down on the loan during this time. When grandma passes one day, Steph and I will then have a decision to make about what to do with this home, but that isn't something that we have to evaluate until the time comes.

To this day, this arrangement has worked wonderfully for everyone. It's a prime example of how business deals can be structured so that all parties not only receive a "fair deal", but how both parties can prosper as a result of the deal taking place. While grandma's house does eat into our monthly budget that we worked so hard to free up, our money is now going towards an appreciating real estate asset. It's a hot, small-town market that will one day far exceed any return on our money that we would receive from the stock market. It's also a low-risk asset with steady, exponential growth that we fully understand. Partnering with family members on deals like this isn't for everyone, but sometimes it can work out if all the details are planned out ahead of time and both parties aren't afraid to deal with each other.

As well as this deal is structured, there is one financial mistake that we made during this process. In early 2019, we completed this process with grandma and closed on a house for her. We had just finished paying off Steph's car and now replaced it with a new house note for grandma. We didn't have $20K in our savings account back then until later that year. The only other place we could get that money for a down payment was from our retirement accounts.

Steph and I each had company sponsored retirement accounts that we contributed to each month automatically. As a rule, you are able to borrow against that money any time you like, however it does come with tax penalties and an income adjustment if you fail to make the monthly payment on it OR are no longer employed by your current employer. When you borrow against this money, you can pull out a lump sum that you then pay back in monthly installments to yourself at an agreed upon interest rate. This interest payment goes 100% back into your retirement account, so you are truly only borrowing money from yourself.

The laws around pulling money from your retirement accounts before retirement age are set up fairly well to keep you from touching this money early in life, but it also allows you access to it in case you have a serious life emergency. The HUGE downside to taking money out of these retirement accounts is that it historically costs you WAY more money in the long run especially if you don't immediately re-invest that money into another asset that will keep up with the stock market. The stock market has historically made money for every single person who has invested in it for a time period of more than 20 years with diversified mutual/index funds. To put simply, taking money from your retirement before retirement age will exponentially decrease your net worth upon you turning 65 years old.

Looking back now, the only way we could have made this deal perfect was for us to not borrow against my retirement account. If we could have found a way to scrap together $20K back then, or even borrowed less, it would have been a perfect situation for Steph and I. Instead, we borrowed the full $20K from my retirement account to buy grandma's house. We do not regret this decision because more than likely, grandma's home will perform as good or better than the stock market in the long run. However, we cannot turn back time and fix this mistake either. We could have had the best of both worlds by leaving more money in the stock market AND still buying grandma's house by scraping together some more cash. I hope you do not make this mistake for yourself. It's highly possible that $20K today can equate to a few hundred thousand dollars over 40 years in the stock market. Don't make this mistake! It is almost NEVER a good idea to pull money from your retirement accounts for any reason.

The Lesson

I want to emphasize how this opportunity came into existence in the first place. It wasn't the possums that started this. Everything became possible the day Steph and I paid off our school loans. Both affording another mortgage payment and qualifying for another home mortgage would not have been possible if we still had $800 in monthly minimum student loan payments and $80K in total debt. Our debt-to-income ratio would have been too high if we still had our student loans in 2019. THIS is the true power of paying off debt! By not being a burden to yourself you can actually help other people in real ways. I don't mean just buying groceries for a neighbor who is struggling or buying Christmas presents for the children of a family where the father lost his job. I mean REAL, MAJOR HELP.

Do you know what it would mean to some people for you to buy them a new car when their 250K mile Toyota Camry dies? What about being able to pay the mortgage of a single mother for an entire year as she deals with the death of her husband? Can you imagine the type of impact you can have on someone else's life simply because you have the ability to do such a thing? To create that ability for yourself and for others will set you free in ways you could never imagine. It starts by not being a burden to yourself. It starts by paying off your debts so that your income is free to both help yourself and others along the way.

Can you even imagine a life where you no longer HAVE to go to a job because you don't owe anything to anyone? If your only monthly bills were utilities, groceries, gas, and car insurance, would you not be able to cover those living expenses with a simple part time job? Or better yet, how about the yearly profit you can make off of your retirement account? Then you don't even need that part time job! Does that not sound like true freedom? Did it get lost that everyone should seek to attain this goal for themselves? Even if it takes 40 or 50 years, does this not sound like something worth achieving? Can you imagine how you can help the world after you achieve this for yourself?

Many people go through life thinking that the only way you can get ahead is by screwing over someone else along the way. It's believing that you have to take shortcuts to get ahead, or you have to "get lucky" somehow. What's interesting about this mind set is the people that believe this, will never find themselves getting ahead. They will stay right where they are at. Nobody wants to do business with someone like this. If you do succeed in screwing over someone once or even twice, they will catch on eventually and word will get around about your character (especially with today's social media). It's a horribly negative way to think and other people instinctually don't want to be a part of that once they get to know you.

The true essence of business is something that makes the world a better place for everyone. It's what drives our world to new innovations that improve our lives in ways we can't imagine. While my situation with grandma is very small compared to that, it is still a wonderful example of how things can be improved for everyone. With a little creativity, an opportunity, and a willingness to make it happen the world can be what we want it to be. Grandma has taught me that.

Chapter 12: Mental Instability and Financial Stability

By the summer of 2019, our lives were crazy! Armed with two mortgages and grandma as our semi-tenant, things were still complicated for me. My home life was steady, Steph and I were overall doing well financially and personally, but my work life was an internal train wreck ready to crash at any moment. I'll break down our monthly expenses again so you can see how the new mortgage payment entered into our financial lives:

Monthly Expenses – Summer 2019	
Monthly Paychecks	$8300
Grandma's Rent	$650
Mortgage	-$1800
Utilities + HOA	-$400
Grandma's Mortgage	-$1300
Minimum Student Loan Payment	-$0!
Groceries & Restaurants	-$450
Steph's Car Note	-$0!
Gas & Car Insurance	-$500
Cell Phones, TV & Internet	-$200
Leftover Money	**$4300**

For the first time since 2014, our monthly leftover income had decreased due to paying half of grandma's mortgage. But it didn't matter! We still had over $4K in excess monthly income that we could save or do anything we wanted with! Our next logical step would have been to attack one of the mortgages with this extra income. We could have continued down this path of freeing up more and more of our monthly expenses. That's not what happened, however.

I had made it through three full layoffs at my job. During the first two, I had been so fearful of such a thing happening to me. Too much of my being was wrapped up in what I was doing at my job, like it was something that made me who I was. To have that threatened, scared me to the core. But it also made me have to question who I actually was and who I wanted to be in the future. I could no longer see a future for myself at my employer. I could raise through the ranks as time went on, but I knew this wasn't going to make me any happier. At the heart of it, I couldn't stand the thought of not being in control of my own fate. That I could still be let go at any moment despite how well I was doing, irked me to the bone. Their inability to maintain the workforce that they built up showed me that they cared more about the bottom dollar and their shareholders over their employees. Steph and I no longer needed their paycheck, so why should I continue to care about their success?

After more than 7 years of working for my employer including my time in college, I gave my two weeks' notice to my boss. I remember him being a little taken aback by this. I was a high performing employee, especially over the last year, things were going well for my project, yet I no longer wished to work there anymore for some reason. I didn't hide the fact that I no longer needed the paycheck that the job provided me with, as good as it was. He didn't have a clue about my personal life or what Steph and I had recently achieved financially. Yet, I can distinctly remember him thinking I had won the lottery, or something similar based on the way I politely declined his attempts to have me stay on at least another month instead of only another two weeks.

I hope the irony doesn't escape you. After three layoffs with 10% workforce reductions, ultimately it was me that decided to part ways with my employer. After all my fear of being let go, I suddenly made them all come true by letting myself go!

Since 2016, when the first layoffs occurred, something stirred inside of me that helped me discover who I really was, what I have the potential to be, and what I am put on this Earth to do. I had figured out that it WASN'T building oil field equipment, but it was a tough 7 years to figure that out. I'm just glad I didn't waste any more time there than I already had. By 2019, my brain was completely fried. To even think about giving another year of my mental capacity to my employer seemed like too much for me to handle. To make that commute for one more week was not something I could do. To be the person I had to be at my job for one more minute was a horribly negative emotion that I no longer cared to be.

The freedom I felt driving away from that parking garage on my last day just about brought tears to my eyes. My reaction that day left no doubt in my mind that I had made the right decision. Steph supported me through it all, but she also had to put up with all my crap in the years leading up to this decision. It's how I know I have the best wife in the world.

By the end of the summer in 2019, our financial lives had drastically shifted. From someone who has always been incredibly grateful for the extraordinary amount of leftover income Steph and I generated for ourselves from 2014-2019, I can tell you that I don't miss that steady income for one minute. Our combined incomes during those years set a financial foundation for ourselves that we will benefit from for the rest of our lives. That income taught us how to live on a budget, how to pay off debt, how to save and invest diligently, and how to search for opportunities to be generous. I am both grateful and angry with the way in which my former employer allowed me the opportunity to learn these lessons for myself. They were hard lessons, but they will one day make Steph and I millionaires.

The craziest thing about all of this is that the world works in mysterious coincidences. About a month after I was no longer working at my regular job, an opportunity presented itself to Steph at her hospital. Steph had gotten to the point where she felt like she mastered her latest nursing position. Her hospital was expanding, and her managers had taken notice of her accomplishments over the last few years. She was encouraged to apply for a leadership position as a nurse manager in order to open a new unit that had been built. While her interview process was arduous, she was ultimately offered the new nurse manager position in the late summer of 2019. She was nervous, energetic, and excited to be starting a new role, but the fact that this significant pay bump happened for her at almost the same time I left my job is quite the coincidence.

Here are our finances broken down during for the late summer of 2019. This was after Steph took her new position and after I quit my job. 2019 was the year of change for us, and our monthly budget showed it! Steph's new salary was right at $100K per year including a one-time yearly bonus (not included below). After taxes, retirement contributions and health insurance were deducted for both of us, the following is what our monthly expenses looked like:

Monthly Expenses – Summer 2019	
Steph's Monthly Paychecks	$5000
Grandma's Rent	$650
Mortgage	-$1800
Utilities + HOA	-$400
Grandma's Mortgage	-$1300
Minimum Student Loan Payment	-$0!
Groceries & Restaurants	-$450
Steph's Car Note	-$0!
Gas & Car Insurance	-$500
Cell Phones, TV & Internet	-$200
Leftover Money	**$1000**

The Lesson

The drop from $4300 to $1000 per month in leftover income was significant for us in 2019. However, it wasn't the end of the world as you can see. Thanks to Steph's new management position, we were still able to pay all our bills with ease and have $1000 leftover as extra income per month. From a financial perspective, it obviously made more sense for me to continue working my job. However, from a personal relationship and mental stability perspective, I would have given up more than $3300 per month to have a wonderful relationship with my wife and be mentally healthy.

From a work perspective, my employer wasn't valuing their employees as much as they had in the past, especially after the price of oil went down. For me to deal with possible future layoffs after 2018, my workload increasing due to fewer people around, company moral and culture in the gutter, and my commute being close to an hour each way; it was more than I cared to handle, especially now that I didn't have to. So, when things aren't working, you change them! And so, we did! Over 5 years, we got our monthly expenses down far enough to not depend on my employer any longer.

After making these decisions both financially and personally for ourselves, I've realized this decision coincides a lot with couples who want to have one parent stay home with their child (or children). Many times, couples are going from two incomes to one while one person stays home full time while the other goes to work. One parent gets to experience all the joys of getting to see their child grow on a daily basis at the expense of making money for their household. Is making more money more important than watching your child grow up? It's both a personal and financial question. No one can answer this question except for you because your life is your own. Both answers are correct because no matter what you choose, you will find a way to make things work if that's what you truly want.

In our case, Steph did not deserve to have to put up with my bitterness caused by my work life. It wasn't fair for me to press that upon her. So, removing $3300 of extra income per month from our household was well worth what we gained in our relationship. I would do it again in a heartbeat. Sometimes the decisions we make for our lives are more important than money. That was our answer during this time in our lives.

Chapter 13: Remodeling, Real Estate & Opportunity

During the late summer and early fall of 2019, I spent 3-4 months remodeling my aunt's house in the Houston area. The week after I quit my job, I started working for her to completely update her house. The remodel skills Steph and I had learned on the weekends over the last few years had paid off in a big way. Our skills and tooling had grown to the point where I could definitely make a living as a general construction contractor if I wanted to. YouTube was a key teacher in learning about everything we needed to know from plumbing, electrical, painting, framing, tiling, and general woodworking. YouTube plus the experience we gained from doing these projects in our own house made us unstoppable! The things we couldn't do, we found licensed professionals to accomplish the work needed.

After I quit my job, I found that my attitude on life almost immediately improved because it felt like I held my destiny in my hands. My aunt's house was built in the 80's and was in serious need of just about everything to update it. In her own life, I think she was at a loss of what to do about her home which put her in a difficult position regarding her mental and physical health. Couple that with her high stress daily job and she was most likely going through something similar to what I had just been through over the last few years at my work. I think we connected in that way, and it was beneficial for both of us. My newfound lifted weight gave me an attitude of almost bubbly positivity; something I had never experienced before when going to work. I'm absolutely sure my attitude rubbed off on my aunt over the months I was at her house working.

There are many lessons I took away from remodeling my aunt's house technically, socially and professionally. All of them were overall positive and personally rewarding by the time I finished her house in the fall of 2019. On top of finishing that project, my aunt carries a much more positive outlook on life to this day. I like to partially take credit for this although I understand it was HER that changed her own way of thinking. It can be a dangerous road to work for your family members, however in this case it turned out very well for both of us because we set guidelines from the beginning and worked very hard to maintain them during the project.

After completing this project, my remodel skills definitely improved significantly. Doing something every day for 4 months, Monday-Friday, 8-5 will do that for you. However, after I completed this job, I didn't have any other major projects lined up to move into. I had been learning a lot about real estate during my long commutes to my previous job as well as the daily drives to my aunt's house, so I was looking for an opportunity down the real estate career path. Sometimes when you are able to keep an open mind with your eyes wide open, things can happen around you in your favor. After a few months, something presented itself to Steph and I which was unexpected.

We had noticed our elderly neighbors directly across the street from us no longer were home anymore. Occasionally somebody would come by like a pest control person and the lawn people, but outside of that we didn't notice anybody getting the mail on a daily basis. Steph and I have always been friendly with our immediate neighbors no matter where we live, so I began asking around as to what had happened to the elderly couple across the street from us. It turned out that the husband had died within the last year and the wife had recently moved into an assisted living facility. This explained why the house was vacant.

At the encouragement of a neighbor, I wrote a letter to the family of the elderly couple letting them know that Steph and I might be interested in purchasing their home if they were ever looking to sell it. I let them know we lived directly across the street if they ever wanted to talk, and I left my contact information on the note. A few weeks later I received a call from the daughter of the elderly couple who had gotten my note and wanted to talk more about possibly selling the house! I was absolutely thrilled! We scheduled a day to meet in order for Steph and I to walk through the house and meet their family. It was a fantastic situation!

If you have ever been involved in a real estate transaction, you may be aware that sometimes things can get sticky during the process. There is definitely a reason that it's a good idea to have realtors involved in any real estate transaction. However, in the state of Texas, realtors or lawyers are not required to be involved if both parties are competent to handle the transaction themselves. Only a title company is necessary for you to complete the transaction. Going this route can save a seller up to 6% from the sale price of the home, which is a significant amount of money. As it turns out, the daughter of the elderly couple was married to a real estate lawyer. They were confident to move forward with us without using a realtor. Steph and I were stepping outside our comfort zone a bit, but with some discussion we formed a plan and decided to go for it!

Working with the daughter (Susan) of the elderly couple, we agreed to keep things simple. Steph and I had been through the buying and selling of our homes multiple times. The process seemed very straight forward to us. Susan agreed not to list her parent's home on the open market, and we discussed that we wanted to maintain a positive relationship with her and her family by not getting into a bunch of negotiations. We agreed to call an appraiser to give a true market value of the home based on recent sales in the neighborhood that the appraiser provided. The appraiser provided a full report and we split the cost of the appraisal which was $400 back then. The home was valued at $190K which Steph and I agreed was a fair price based on its condition (it was in a mostly original 1970's style and needed a new HVAC system badly).

With the price sorted out, I spent numerous days learning about residential contracts. The Texas Real Estate Commission (TREC) provides a wonderful standard contract to people looking to buy and sell homes in Texas. While it is frowned upon for regular people to use this contract without a realtor, this form can be downloaded by anyone online and filled out as they please. Using the completed templates we had from buying and selling of our previous homes, I set about filling out the contract in this manner. We filled out a few additional addendums that were necessary for the contract and Poof! The deal got done!

As part of the plan, Steph and I knew that we could sell our current house for a small profit if we listed it on the market. As I said, we had worked to remodel it significantly over the last 2.5 years. On top of regular appreciation, we had forced the value of our home up by making some significant changes that didn't cost us much money. The most noteworthy projects we did were replace all the flooring in the house with a combination of tile and laminate, painted the entire inside, remodeled both bathrooms, added a covered patio in the backyard, and modernized the stairs. We did almost all the work ourselves which is really where our profit came from. It was our sweat equity.

As a part of the overall plan, we went ahead and listed our current house on the market. It took a little over three months for our house to sell which was an average amount of time for any home during 2019 and early 2020. Susan was wonderfully patient with us during this time, and we are eternally grateful to her and her family for selling us her parent's home. By April of 2020 Steph and I were moving all of our furniture slowly across the street one truck load at a time! The final numbers for the sale of our old home were a sales price of $299K which meant Steph and I profited $16K after subtracting all our material costs over 2.5 years. Not too bad for two people who had never remodeled a home before! We were thrilled by the whole ordeal!

The idea of Steph and I downsizing our life was exactly what we were doing once again. This would now be the second time we were going through this, but this time, without the NEED to do it because of our fear of me losing my job. After all was settled, we traded a $299K house for $190K house, saving over $100K off the mortgage! AND ALL WE DID WAS MOVE ACROSS THE STREET! On top of this wonderful scenario, interest rates slightly decreased yet again during this time period for a 30-year mortgage! Somehow, we had found a way to significantly decrease our living expenses by noticing an opportunity literally across the street. The world is a crazy place!

To summarize, our monthly payment for the new house ended up right at $1400 per month including taxes, insurances, PMI, principal and interest. We again put 5% down on a 30-year conventional loan like we had for our previous primary houses.

The Lesson

This was our first real estate transaction where we had the confidence to buy a home without a realtor. Being able to save the seller having to pay any realtor fees was a big help to Susan and her family. While it was a little scary managing a major home purchase ourselves, everything is always a little scary the first time you do it. Remember, we had been through the selling process twice and the home buying process three times leading up to the purchase of this home. That absolutely gave us some confidence.

What provided us even more confidence was that we had just paid off Steph's car loan and our student loans the previous year. Our living expenses were already low, so we weren't concerned about being able to afford anything. Buying the house across the street felt more like icing on the cake to further improve our lives. The correct way to think about this was that it was a good opportunity if it worked out, but it wasn't the end of our world if it didn't for some reason.

Not using a realtor to purchase this home was also one of the first times Steph and I "went against the cultural grain" so to speak. All of our friends, family and everyone we knew used realtors to buy a home on the open market. Our culture advertises that trying to complete a transaction like this on your own is not only risky, but complicated. After going through this ourselves, I can honestly say that I disagree with the "cultural norm" on this topic. Don't misunderstand me, I absolutely believe that realtors are valuable in the real estate industry, but they are more valuable to some people over others depending on an individual's skill set and experience. To highlight the complexity of this topic, I'll make this final statement in an effort to clarify my opinion. Steph and I WILL use a realtor for a future home buying or selling transaction when we need to, BUT when the opportunity presents itself to remove the realtor from the process, we will absolutely take advantage of that. We will attempt to keep realtors out of our lives but acknowledge that we will have to play along with the "cultural norm" if we want a particular piece of real estate in the future.

Every person and every couple will form their own opinions on this topic. It's important to seek to understand your individual point of view before buying or selling a home. These were simply our observations after going through numerous buying and selling transactions with realtors over the years, compared to one transaction without them.

Chapter 14: Covid Hit

B y April of 2020 our monthly finances had changed quite a bit from the previous year for multiple reasons. Not only had we moved houses to lower our monthly payment, but Steph also got a slight raise at work due to market adjustments and her yearly pay bump. To counteract this, I can remember being annoyed because our TV/Internet bill went up a little even after I called and threatened to change providers. These services were slightly more expensive in 2020 no matter what I did, but the result was an increase to our leftover money by $250 per month. Moving across the street also lowered our monthly expenses by about $400, totaling $650 per month in all from the previous summer. Once again, the most important aspect was that we INCREASED our leftover money per month compared to the summer of 2019:

Monthly Expenses – Spring of 2020	
Steph's Monthly Paychecks	$5300
Grandma's Rent	$650
Mortgage	-$1400
Utilities + HOA	-$400
Grandma's Mortgage	-$1300
Minimum Student Loan Payment	-$0!
Groceries & Restaurants	-$450
Steph's Car Note	-$0!
Gas & Car Insurance	-$500
Cell Phones, TV & Internet	-$250
Leftover Money	**$1650**

While the spring of 2020 was crazy for Steph and I, it was also a scary time in the world. March, April, and May were particularly scary months from a global pandemic perspective due to Covid-19. Steph was now a nurse manager at a major hospital system in our community. Her work life was stressed to the max worrying about all her employees and the particularly sick patients that she had on her floor. Most people that were hospitalized for Covid at her hospital did recover, but many of them didn't. The elderly as well as patients with pre-existing sicknesses were the highest risk for developing complications due to Covid. To sum up the difficulty of this time, I can remember Steph telling me about her boss's boss (the Chief Nursing Officer of the hospital) shedding tears of empathy and frustration at the situation that Covid caused for all patients, the families of patients, the staff, and families of the staff. Steph had never seen one of the main leaders of her hospital show such emotion towards any situation before. Covid-19 will probably be one of the worst global pandemic situations to hit hospitals for at least the next 50 years.

Despite this horrible event, Steph and I did our best to maintain a peaceful lifestyle at home. Steph's duties at work heavily increased during this time, but we maintained our normal working schedules for the most part. Luckily our new house provided me a way to fully work from home during the rest of 2020. Our new house was older, built in 1978, and was mostly in original condition. When we bought it, we absolutely knew we were going to remodel the entire thing, more so than our previous house. We had the skills to do it now, and we had put some extra cash back in our pockets from the sale of our previous home. Not only did we pocket the $16K in profit; we also recovered some of the equity that we had built up. We bought the house for $235K, sold it for $299K, but we only owed about $213K on the mortgage when we sold it in 2020. Our closing costs for the sale of our home (because we did use a realtor to sell it on the open market) were about $12K. We had found a realtor who agreed to list our house for a $5K commission fee instead of the full 3% which saved us close to $4K. So, at the closing of our house, our bank account received $74K in funds ($299K - $12K - $213K). We did have to turn around and put 5% down on the new house, which was $9.5K but that obviously wasn't an issue after we deposited $74K into it!

All in all, we now had about $65K in additional cash that we could help to fully remodel the new house. It was a fantastic scenario! On top of this, this cash was over and beyond our regular savings which we always kept between $10-20K just in case something bad happened in our lives. So, in the early summer of 2020, we had just over $80K in our bank account!

I want to pause here to highlight the importance of this. For a poor kid growing up used to keeping his high school checking account between $200-300 dollars, this was crazy! EIGHTY THOUSAND DOLLARS IS AN UNHEARD-OF AMOUNT OF MONEY FOR SOMEONE OF MY UPBRINGING! To make things even better, it's an astronomical amount of money WHEN YOU DON'T NEED IT. Steph and I could have lived off this money for an entire 18 months if she would have been fired from her job the next day. To be able to think about money in this way was a completely new concept to us. We always believed that at least one of us would have to maintain a regular job to be able to eat and pay our basic bills, but that was no longer the case! Can you even fathom what your life could be if you didn't have to go to a regular job every day? What would you do? What would you want to accomplish? Who would you want to help? This is a wonderful question for all humans to ask themselves.

Having $80K in our bank account fundamentally changed the way we thought about money. It was a turning point for us because we eliminated our need for either of us to HAVE to have a regular job in order to survive. Over the course of 2020, our minds exited the survival aspect of thinking about money and shifted to a thriving mind set where anything is possible. Anything is possible because WE WERENT WORRIED ABOUT SIMPLY SURVIVING ANYMORE. While this money would technically only last us 18 months with our current expenses, that easily felt like an extraordinary amount of time for us to accomplish anything we wanted. Having this much money (or more) in our bank account shifted our mind set in a very positive way. It was like lifting a weight off our shoulders that we didn't even know was there in the first place.

Luckily, having a nice big pile of cash in our bank account was a wonderful thing to have going into a global pandemic. While going to the grocery store each week was more stressful than previously, we were never afraid of not having enough money to buy the things we needed. Even if those things were more expensive. We knew we could afford anything we needed during the pandemic, and that was a wonderful security blanket in our lives during this time.

After the first quarter of 2020, many businesses had to shut down or stop operating due to the fear of spreading Covid. For us, this turned out to be the absolute best time for me to get to work remodeling our new house. There is nothing better than working at home when the world is shut down. Steph and I spent the rest of 2020 getting our hands dirty like we never had before. Everyday, I treated working on our house as if I was going to a regular job. Up by 7 AM and cleaning up by 4 PM in time to start making dinner for the evening. The progress we made on the house was astounding by maintaining this working schedule.

Here is a quick summary of all the projects we took on in order to remodel this house. Two and half bathrooms were fully gutted with a huge walk-in shower installed for the primary bath. All the first-floor flooring was updated to beautiful wood look tile. A brand-new kitchen complete with new cabinets, granite, backsplash and appliances. The whole house was painted both inside and outside. Two new HVAC (Heating Ventilation & Air Condition) systems were installed. Three major walls were removed on the first floor to create an open concept. The stairway was modernized, and a major front yard landscaping project got completed. The only things we didn't do ourselves was paint the outside of the house, install the new HVAC units, install the cabinets and granite, and some drywall work. Outside of those things, all plumbing, electrical, painting, and tiling was fair game for us to complete ourselves. The house ended up turning out fantastic! Our skills throughout this house vastly improved once again simply because we were doing it all the time.

By May of 2021, over one year later, we had finished remodeling every aspect of the house. The rest of the world had paused over the summer and fall of 2020, but those months turned out to be some of our hardest working months ever. Also, during 2020 the real estate market hit the pause button in a significant way. Not many houses went up for sale during this time in our area, but it wasn't too much of an issue because not many people were looking to buy a home during these months either. The world was pandemic stricken. In the fall and winter of 2020, that absolutely changed!

An Average Guy's Journey to Becoming a Millionaire

It felt like over night the housing market in our area boomed in a way that Steph and I had never seen. We knew that hot markets like in California or New York could experience huge boom and bust cycles, but the Houston area had always been largely immune to these things. Homes in the Houston area have historically grown at a very, slow and steady pace within the last 50 years, despite what other parts of the country are experiencing. That data became insignificant at end of 2020 and into 2021. Once the pandemic fears subsided, the real estate market and the general economy boomed as a result of many things.

The house we had purchased only a little over a year ago for $190K was now valued at $345K by our estimations! After realizing this, Steph and I decided that it made sense for us to sell our house again. Within 3 days after listing, we had a full price cash offer on our house as a result of the housing boom. It was nuts! All in, we had put about $42K in material and labor into the house, not including our own labor. So, in July of 2021 we walked away from the closing table with a check for over $143K! If these numbers don't blow your mind, I'm not sure what will because they absolutely keep me stunned to this day. We owed about $178K on the mortgage in July of 2021, so our total profit was right at $101K including realtor fees and closing costs of about $24K ($345K sale price - $24K closing costs - $42K materials and labor - $178K mortgage = $101K). For us to be able to accomplish this, especially during a global pandemic, is something I will never get over. These are extraordinary numbers! Nothing could have prepared us for this kind of achievement.

The Lesson

Steph and I had every intention of living in our new house for a very long time when we bought it in 2020. The monthly mortgage payment was low, we owed under $180K total on the mortgage, and the house was plenty big enough to accommodate any future family growing plans. However, the real estate market post Covid in late 2020 and early 2021 was something that absolutely took our breath away. We had never seen housing prices explode like that. Our friends and older family members had never seen anything like it during their lives. When the world emerged from the post Covid scare after being locked in their homes isolated for six months, new buyers came in floods into the housing market looking for a piece of real estate to buy. Couple this with interest rates that were below 3% for all of 2020, plus a population exodus from places like California where the cost of living was so high; it created the perfect storm for the housing market to explode in Houston and Texas in general.

Steph and I unknowingly put ourselves in an extreme position of strength without knowing what the future would hold in early 2020. We absolutely loved the house we had worked so hard to remodel, but we couldn't ignore that cashing in on our efforts could set us up in the future more so than we ever dreamed. While it was hard to let that house go, we knew we weren't making a bad decision by taking advantage of what the real estate market was presenting to us. In addition to this, Steph and I had been talking about her going back to school to get her master's degree in nursing. Selling the house seemed like a wise decision in order to be able to afford to pay cash for all of Steph's graduate degree. After all the student loan nonsense we had been through, going back into debt was absolutely something we were NOT going to do.

The buying and selling of our houses in 2020 and 2021 were a major turning point in our lives. It was during these years that we began to view money differently in our minds. The weight of simply surviving was lifted. It was a burden that we never knew was on our shoulders. It's for this reason that I highly encourage you to do everything you can to get to this point in your financial life. However you do it, either by using Dave Ramsey, your church group, or simply your own grit; getting to this point in your financial life will set you up for the rest of your life. It's the point where the ball rolling down the hill can almost never be stopped no matter what you do. To pay off all your student loans, not have a car payment, not have any other personal or credit card loans, and to have a back up fund with $10-20K to cover your life emergencies will pave the way for you to become a millionaire. You will think about your life differently. You will think about your children's lives differently. And overall, you will be a happier person because you don't owe anyone anything and your burden for survival is lifted. It's a mindset that will cause you to make better decisions for the rest of your life, and I truly hope that you find a way to achieve this no matter the cost in your life.

Chapter 15: Where We Are Today

As of writing this in the summer of 2022, our lives are wonderful! Steph decided to go back to school for a dual graduate program where she will receive both her Master's in Nursing as well as an MBA. She will complete this in the summer of 2023. The best part about it is that her current employer will pay for about 30% of the total cost of the degree with the rest coming completely from us in cash. NEVER AGAIN TO STUDENT LOANS!

After selling our house in the summer of 2021, we moved into another house in the same neighborhood two months later. While it was easy to sell the last house, buying another one turned out to be more difficult than we anticipated. A booming housing market is a wonderful thing for a seller, but not so much for buyer. We ended up buying another house needing a ton of remodel work for $320K. We chose to over bid the asking price of $315K because there were already 3 other offers on the property before we got there. For the first time in our lives, we were able to present a wonderfully strong offer to the sellers in the form of a full 20% down payment, no inspection or option periods, no warranties, and a closing date of their choosing. This was enough for us to win the house despite a crazy housing market.

Before you think we are crazy for doing all those things, please consider everything I have told you leading up to this point in our lives. Every family is different in how they assess risk in their life. Steph and I already knew we wanted to fully remodel any house we were going to buy, so forgoing inspections is not a big deal for us any longer because we tear apart any house we get our hands on anyway. On top of this, we have enough experience to identify houses with major problems like foundation and structure damage to stay away from. As far as over bidding the price, this turned out to work out in our favor as time passed over the next year. The housing market continued to increase in our area during 2021 and 2022, so much so that the current value of the house just one year later is very close to $400K. I would agree that overbidding on a piece of real estate is not always a good idea, but it worked out for us in this case. Steph and I will not seek to over bid on any houses in the future unless a special circumstance presents itself. In this case, the house we bought was a floor plan we always wanted, and it needed exactly the kind of remodel work that we now seem to specialize in.

To sum up our financials on this newest house, we bought it for $320K while putting $64K down to avoid private mortgage insurance. The monthly payment is right at $1800 per month because we locked in an interest rate of 2.75% on a 30-year mortgage. That is absolutely the lowest interest rate we have ever gotten since 2014. Since the spring of 2020, our monthly expenses haven't changed dramatically, but I'll summarize them one last time for you to compare. Steph has received multiple pay bumps since 2020 as a result of her efforts during Covid as well as from her commitment to pursue higher education levels.

Monthly Expenses – Summer of 2022	
Steph's Monthly Paychecks	$7000
Grandma's Rent	$650
Mortgage	-$1800
Utilities + HOA	-$500
Grandma's Mortgage	-$1300
Minimum Student Loan Payment	-$0!
Groceries & Restaurants	-$450
Steph's Car Note	-$0!
Gas & Car Insurance	-$500
Cell Phones, TV & Internet	-$250
Leftover Money	**$2850**

Most of this leftover income goes directly into paying for Steph's graduate degrees as well as remodeling the newest house. While this is a wonderful cash flow per month, this leftover money is not what brings us peace any longer. The reason we know our lives are going to be okay is because even if Steph lost her job tomorrow, we once again have a savings account in excess of $75K. We could survive off this money once again for over 18 months with our current bills without either of us needing to get a regular job. This is the peace we have in our lives. This is one of the ways I know we will achieve millionaire status one day.

Since the late summer of 2021, we took the next step in our financial lives in order to achieve millionaire status in the future. I wish I could tell you it's some secret, but it's not. It's actually super boring. All we did was start automatically paying $1000 every month on our mortgage. The only liabilities that Steph and I have left that are stopping us from becoming millionaires are our home mortgages. At this moment, based on the values of both properties, if we were to pay them both off, we would be millionaires. We owe $390K mortgage debt between both houses. However, the combined value of both homes are well in excess of $650K.

While this contributes to our net worth, paying these houses off is our next step to becoming millionaires without having to worry about what the outside world will do. I'm not relying on the stock market to make us millionaires or our next home flip project. I'm not even considering that the values of our homes increase any over the next ten years. I'm only banking on being able to pay $1000 or more per month for the next however many years in order to reduce our mortgage liabilities. That's it. It's that simple. It's easy, straight forward and simple to follow. Everything Steph and I have been through to pay off student loans and our cars have led us to this point where simplicity each month is the key.

I hope you one day get to feel this relief of simplicity in your life like we do. If each month you can make progress to pay down your liabilities, you too can achieve this! All you have to do is stay focused and not be distracted by the new ideas and people that come into your life. Make a plan, stick to it, and get it done! That's how you become a millionaire!

The Lesson

Automatically contributing any money towards something you want is a great tool to carry around in your tool bag. In the same way that your employer automatically deducts your retirement and health insurance, you can do the same for anything you choose. The trick is to find a way to ensure that the money you want to allocate doesn't hit your bank account. Or if it does hit your bank account, set up an extra automatic draw the day after you get paid one time a month so that money is sucked out of your account the day after you get paid. The ability to set something on autopilot so that you aren't wasting brain power on it any longer is a great tool for everyone. Especially if it relates to money. The idea is that money in your bank account gives you the temptation to spend it, but money that you never see can't be spent.

I don't have to think about our extra $1000 going towards the mortgage every month anymore. It just happens and we automatically add $1000 to our net worth each month by reducing our mortgage debt. No matter what happens around me, I know this will happen regardless of what I do. So, this is another way that I can make sure that Steph and I achieve millionaire status one day. It's one more way that the ball gains momentum downhill.

Based on our current trajectory, I estimate that Steph and I will achieve millionaire status within the next 5-10 years. That is my estimation that comes from me tracking our net worth over the last few years. I can see how much our net worth grows each year, and therefore, I can guess what that number might be ten years from now. While we aren't relying on the stock market or the real estate market, the reality is that both of those things will probably help us to achieve millionaire status over the next ten years. This is why I encourage you to start tracking your net worth. It will highlight where you currently are and help you to estimate when you can be a millionaire! As long as you focus on growing your net worth, a good rule of thumb is that you can expect your net worth to double every seven years. This only happens if you work on it though. It does not happen automatically if you keep going into debt.

Parting Words

The goal of this book is simple. It is my hope that this story gives you hope to believe that you can become a millionaire. Anyone from any working class, living anywhere across the United States, making any amount of income CAN become a millionaire. That is the message I hope to convey to you by sharing our story.

At heart I am an American patriot. I love my country. I was not a veteran, nor have I ever served the public in any professional way. But my dad did surely teach me to take off your hat and cover your heart when the national anthem starts playing. We are truly blessed to be able to live in the greatest country in the world.

People risk their lives every day in an attempt to make it into this country. Crossing boarders, faking documents, and committing crimes are normal activities that we do not see every day, but they do indeed happen as people fight to make it into the United States. Why do they do this? Why put everything at risk to try and change the nation in which you reside?

Because this is the greatest country in the world. I truly believe that and I hope you do too. The world has about 7 billion people. If you are one of the lucky 350 million people who live in the United States, among the 5% of the world's population that was born here, you are blessed.

Now what makes this country the best in the world? In my opinion, it's for the ability of anyone to be able to safely and legally provide for their family. To be able to build wealth and pass it on to their next generation. To change their family tree forever. To leave a legacy where each generation after the next is better off than the previous. To be clear, "better off" translates to "having more money". It's that simple. What other place in the world is better to achieve this? This is also referred to as the American dream, where anyone can become anything including having however much money they desire.

List of Books Which Helped Begin Our Financial Journey

The following list of books helped me on educating myself in the ways of financial literacy. Read together, they form a powerful set of tools that allows anyone to achieve becoming a millionaire. The books below are listed in order of importance for my life. If you are unsure of which to read first, start at the top of the list and work your way down. Each one of these books will help you in some way.

1. Rich Dad Poor Dad by Robert Kiyosaki
2. The Richest Man in Babylon by George Samuel Clason
3. Think and Grow Rich by Napoleon Hill
4. The Millionaire Next Door by Thomas J. Stanley
5. The E Myth Revisited by Michael E. Gerber
6. The Total Money Makeover by Dave Ramsey
7. Baby Steps Millionaires by Dave Ramsey
8. Bigger Pockets Real Estate Podcast

I've listened to hundreds of real estate podcasts by Bigger Pockets. I learned so much about real estate during my previous long commutes to work. These podcasts are fantastic for anyone wanting to learn about real estate from the beginning.

Quotes & Facts That Have Served Me Well

These quotes, phrases and facts help to keep me motivated when I read them from time to time. I hope they may bring you some measure of clarity, inspiration or motivation anytime you need it in your life:

1) Boring investing leads to an exciting life.

2) Making more money is like lighting candles all around you. One person making more money facilitates other people around you to make money. The opposite way to think about this idea is to believe that you must somehow take advantage of others in order to get ahead. Trying to take from others will only get you so far. That way of life will eventually run out keeping you poor all along the way.

3) There is no limit on the income you can generate for yourself. Coupon cutting and cutting back on spending helps but can only go so far. Saving 10% on your total monthly budget is helpful but is insignificant

compared to doubling or tripling your income every 3 years.

4) The human brain isn't fully developed until an average age of 25 years old. (Meaning teenage brains are not fully able think with their prefrontal cortex, the rational part of the brain to make decisions) Many major life decisions for people are made before the age of 25 like going to college, getting married, having kids, and setting a person's perceived view of the world. To be President of the United States, you must be 35 years or older. (Requirement of the Constitution since George Washington). Think about that.

5) The only true lesson to take away from going to college is to learn how to think. To learn how to learn through the act of learning new things over and over again, until you believe that you are capable of learning anything. Otherwise, college is useless. It's essentially a hugely overpriced set of accountability partners in the form of multiple professors, other students and the academic institution. All professions on this Earth can be learned by someone willing to teach you even if you don't have a piece of paper to prove what you know.

6) You are what you think, just like you are what you eat. You are what you think you are and want to be. The mind is a powerful thing. If you believe you can never get a higher paying job or get married or find a

boyfriend or can't exit the endless cycle of work/sleep/work/sleep, then you will never have any of those things. You must first believe in yourself as a first step. It requires true bravery to do this. (My brother struggles with this 100%. I hope one day he will be able to do this). This is why Disney World is one of my favorite places. The first time I went there, the "lesson" I took away from that trip was that dreams CAN become real. My TRUE happiness is achievable. Anything is possible, just look at that place! How can such a place be real? Built in the middle of a swamp? Look so clean? Have all the staff be so happy? It literally feels like that place shouldn't exist but it does.

7) Some people will always be workers, never bosses. Mostly the people not reading a book like this will always be workers. To have the vision and goal for something better for yourself is important and something that many people feel as if they can never achieve. To expand your mind and have self confidence in yourself to progress forward with difficult goals is something that many people never choose to do in their life. It's this more than anything that separates bosses from workers, and high-income earners from lower ones.

8) If you always plan to work for someone else your whole life, you will have an issue building generational

wealth. It is absolutely possible to become a millionaire working for a period of many years for an employer. But in an effort to multiply your income more quickly you will eventually have to work for yourself in order to surpass the 5-10 millionaire mark.

9) The amount of money you make is almost a direct correlation to the value you bring to the marketplace. And it's not connected to your personal value as a human being on this earth.

10) The definition of intelligence is how you view it. Our culture likes to reinforce intelligence as something you have or don't have. Are you smart or not smart? People who view smartness as something you are born with, or something you are God given are more likely to be among the poorer people in society. When you are able to view intelligence more so as a living breathing entity that exists in your head to continually grow and evolve; as something that must be constantly fed and adapted to gain more useful skills for yourself and for society as a whole. That is a more dynamic definition of intelligence. It is something much more difficult to describe with the English written language. If you can learn to view intelligence in this dynamic manner, you are much more likely to become a millionaire. Going to college and seeking the higher levels of education

past a high school diploma can unlock this shift in people's minds of the definition of intelligence I have found.

11) To waste an additional minute doing something you don't like, no matter how high the paycheck, is not worth it in the long run. While everyone has to find a way to eat and survive, working towards doing what you want AND being paid for it is one of the keys to a happy life. Even if you have been a doctor for 30 years and no longer care to be one anymore, you will more than likely do better for the world and for yourself by following your passion. Do not waste your time.

12) Doing nothing sometimes requires diligence and perseverance in itself. As an example, go get $30K in your bank account. Let it sit there and do nothing for one whole year. The act of letting a big pile of money sit in your bank account without spending any of it is a difficult act on its own. Give it try! It's not easy!

13) Being rich is walking into an outlet mall and being able to buy anything you want. Being wealthy means going to the same mall, still being able to buy anything you want, but walking out the front door without anything in your hands. Wealth is a mindset. Being rich means you just have money.

Thank You!

Thanks for reading! If you enjoyed this book please consider leaving a review on Amazon for me! Amazon reviews are the key to spreading the word so that everyone can be a millionaire! My goal is to help as many people achieve millionaire status as possible. It can only happen if more and more people believe that they can actually achieve it. Too many people do not have the confidence in themselves to believe that they can or deserve to be a millionaire. Amazon reviews are one small way to challenge that way of thinking!

Your review will definitely be seen by me! I read all reviews no matter what, so please consider leaving me a review! Thank you!

Made in the USA
Columbia, SC
14 November 2022